# THE
# WORLDS OF
# GEORGE R·R·
# MARTIN

For Alfie, in his 18th year.
Go forth, and conquer.

# Quarto

First published in 2024 by Frances Lincoln,
an imprint of The Quarto Group.
One Triptych Place, London, SE1 9SH,
United Kingdom
T (0)20 7700 9000
www.Quarto.com

A catalogue record for this book is available
from the British Library.

ISBN 978-0-7112-8852-2
Ebook ISBN 978-0-7112-8853-9

10 9 8 7 6 5 4 3 2 1

Design by Intercity

Publisher: Philip Cooper
Commissioning Editor: John Parton
Senior Editor: Laura Bulbeck
Deputy Art Director: Isabel Eeles
Cover Design: Daisy Woods
UK Production Director: Angela Graef

Printed in China

FSC
www.fsc.org
MIX
Paper | Supporting
responsible forestry
FSC® C016973

# THE WORLDS OF GEORGE R·R· MARTIN

## THE INSPIRATIONS BEHIND
## GAME OF THRONES

Tom Huddleston

FRANCES
LINCOLN

108

Part Three
# WEST & SOUTH

146

Part Four
# ESSOS

Introduction

# A THOUSAND LIVES

In the many realms of modern fantasy there is only one true king, and his name is George Raymond Richard Martin.

The story of how a dockworker's son from Bayonne, New Jersey, came to dominate fantasy, both in literature and on the screen, is almost as unlikely as one of his tales. Raised amid the ruins of his maternal family's once-thriving empire, on the shores of the evocatively named Kill Van Kull, Martin would grow up in relative penury, the eldest of three children and the only son. But his love of stories – first superhero comics, then science fiction, horror, fantasy and historical epics – would offer more than just a figurative escape from his stifling suburban roots.

From his earliest efforts at writing monster stories to entertain his young neighbours, through his years as a respected short fiction writer, struggling novelist and TV screenwriter, to his life-changing success with 1996's *A Game of Thrones* and its era-defining 2011 small-screen adaptation, Martin's ascent has been slow but steady: an inexorable rise, rather than an overnight revolution. Along the way he has enjoyed the friendship, encouragement and inspiration of countless fellow writers, editors and enthusiasts, becoming a familiar face on the worldwide convention scene and winning numerous Hugo, Locus, Nebula and Emmy awards.

But George R.R. Martin is not just a 'fanboy',[1] as he's happy to call himself. He's also an avid student of history, an enthusiastic traveller, a game-player and a collector, and a keen observer of people, all of which feed directly into his writing. Martin describes *A Game of Thrones* and its sequels – the ongoing series of doorstop novels known collectively as *A Song of Ice and Fire* – as his attempt to 'combine some of the realism of historical fiction with ... the magic and the wonder that the best fantasy has.'[2] And indeed, the novels draw on countless real-world sources, from the Roman fortifications of ancient Britain to the medieval Wars of the Roses, from the eighth-century siege of Constantinople to the thirteenth-century Mongol conquests.

These borrowings from history are never blunt or clumsy – as Martin says, 'I like to use history to flavour my fantasy, to add texture and verisimilitude, but simply rewriting history with the names changed has no appeal for me.'[3] But they are a key element of what makes *A Song of Ice and Fire* so effective, so in this book we'll seek to untangle some of these roots, investigating how and to what extent real history has influenced Martin's work. At the same time, we'll also look at some of Martin's less obvious influences, from the obscure comic-book superhero whose untimely demise would inspire the fate of Ned Stark, to the great science-fiction and fantasy authors whose work made such an impression on the young Martin.

Because, perhaps more than anything else, George R.R. Martin is a reader: a voracious gatherer of knowledge, of experience, of story – and whether that story comes in the form of a four-colour funny book or a hefty account of historical hardship makes no great difference. In the words of the young crannogman Jojen Reed in *A Dance With Dragons* (2011): 'A reader lives a thousand lives before he dies ... The man who never reads lives only one.'[4] This book aims to explore just a handful of the thousand lives of George R.R. Martin – starting, of course, with the real one.

George Raymond Martin (the Richard would be added at age 13, following his Catholic confirmation) was born on 20 September 1948 to longshoreman Raymond Collins Martin – 'Smokey', to his friends – and his wife Margaret Brady Martin, the daughter of a once-wealthy family whose construction business had funded the bustling Brady Dock that lay directly across the street from the low-income housing block where Martin spent most of his childhood. The Great Depression had ruined the Bradys, but their story nonetheless deeply affected the young Martin, who spent his childhood feeling like 'disinherited royalty'[5] – a concept familiar to readers of *A Song of Ice and Fire*.

Growing up in Bayonne was by no means hellish – 'we swung on swings and slid down slides, went wading in the summer and had snowball fights in the winter, climbed trees and rollerbladed.'[6] But young George dreamed of more – a life of excitement like the ones he read about in the *Batman*, *Superman* and *Fantastic Four* comics he adored, and later the 35c sci-fi paperbacks of Robert A. Heinlein, Andre Norton, Jack Vance and countless others. At the very least, he wanted to tell stories of his own, turning out 'scary stories about a monster hunter' that he sold to friends for the princely sum of 1c a page, complete with a 'free dramatic reading'.[7]

Further inspiration arrived in unlikely, amphibious form: a family of turtles purchased from a local pet store and kept in a plastic tank on Martin's writing table. This tank was housed within a toy castle, and, because of this, Martin began to imagine his pets as kings and knights engaged in fierce power struggles. These legends were rarely committed to paper, but 'I acted out all the best bits in my head, the swordfights and battles and betrayals.'[8] If only the half-shelled heroes of Turtle Castle had known what their world-conquering legacy would be.

By the early 1960s, the teenage Martin was caught up in the burgeoning world of fanzines: DIY magazines that were written, printed and sold largely by enthusiastic youths, full of hand-drawn strips, short stories and rants about the world of comics, and personal ads where fans could sell and trade issues. Martin may have been miserable at his new Catholic prep school, the all-boys Marist High, but writing for the fanzines kept him at least partially distracted. Tapping away on his aged typewriter, Martin would churn out tales of masked avengers, skiing superheroes and Garizan: The Mechanical Warrior, an alien brain in a goldfish bowl whose range of robot bodies gave him the power to fight crime. He also captained the school chess team and edited the school paper, *The Shield*, before 'getting thrown off early senior year in a censorship dispute',[9] the exact nature of which remains a mystery.

Martin graduated high school in 1966 and later that year took the Greyhound bus 1,300 km (800 miles) to Evanston,

# 'I'VE ALWAYS WRITTEN. IT'S A DISEASE.'

George R.R. Martin[10]

**LEFT**
Home of House Martin: the wharfs, harbours and industrial sector of Bayonne, New Jersey

**RIGHT**
Con man: George R.R. Martin at the signing table at London's World Science Fiction Convention in 2014

**OPPOSITE**
'The man who passes the sentence should swing the sword': Sean Bean as Ned Stark in HBO's adaptation of Martin's novels

# 'There are three rules for writing a novel. Unfortunately, no one knows what they are.'

W. Somerset Maugham, 'approved' by George R.R. Martin[11]

Illinois, where he'd been accepted onto Northwestern University's prestigious journalism programme. Unavoidable distractions, such as coursework, alcohol and the opposite sex, may have led to a drop-off in productivity. However, a course in Scandinavian history led not just to Martin's first encounter with the great Norse sagas, but to a work of historically inspired short fiction entitled *The Fortress*, whose submission to (and ultimate rejection by) *The American-Scandinavian Review* would be his first brush with professional writing. With its island citadels, grim-faced soldiers and roots in military history, *The Fortress* would join the denizens of Turtle Castle as a distant ancestor to the worlds of Ice and Fire.

In time, Martin would feel confident enough to begin submitting regularly to magazines, though the process would take time and patience: one story, *The Added Safety Factor* – later rewritten by fellow author, George Guthridge, and retitled *Warship* – would garner an extraordinary 42 rejections before being published in *F&SF* magazine in 1979, more than a decade after it was first written. Gradually, Martin's persistence began to pay off. In 1970, having been submitted to the wrong editor and lost for a year behind a filing cabinet, his story *The Hero* was purchased for the princely sum of $94

by *Galaxy* magazine, one of the leading publishers of sci-fi. The following February, at the age of 23, George R.R. Martin was a published writer.

In 1971, having completed a postgraduate journalism course at Northwestern, George R.R. Martin became eligible for the military draft. A staunch opponent of America's war in Vietnam, he refused to join the 156,000 US troops then stationed in the country. 'I applied for conscientious-objector status,' he said later, 'in full belief that I would be rejected, and that I would have a further decision to make: army, jail or Canada. I don't know what I would've done.'[12] But, to his surprise, the request was granted, so in place of military service Martin joined the VISTA programme, a volunteer organization founded by John F. Kennedy as a domestic alternative to the Peace Corps. Working for the Cook County Legal Assistance Fund, Martin would draft press releases and edit newsletters, living in a grand shared house in the Chicago suburbs and spending his free time working on his stories and submissions.

In the coming decade, Martin's writing would become a staple feature of the popular sci-fi magazines, including five stories sold to *Analog Science Fiction and Fact*, then under the editorship of the prolific science-fiction writer Ben Bova.

It was the fourth of these, 1974's *A Song for Lya*, that would bring Martin's work to greater prominence. Inspired by 'the first serious romance of my life',[13] this longer-form story of two human telepaths on an alien planet would win Martin his first Hugo award – for Best Novella in 1975 – and would also lend its title to his first collection, a 1976 paperback compiling the best of his published stories to date.

The following year would finally see the release of George R.R. Martin's first novel. Initially serialized in *Analog* as *After the Festival*, the book ultimately published as *Dying of the Light* would prove a critical rather than a commercial success, rich in alien world-building but rather more contemplative than most mainstream science fiction. Two years later, however, another story would garner Martin his widest audience yet. Initially printed in *Omni* and telling the gruesome story of an exotic animal collector who stumbles upon a voracious, insectoid alien race, *Sandkings* would win Hugo, Nebula and Locus awards, and later be adapted for television as part of 1995's short-lived *Outer Limits* reboot. But it wasn't the only Hugo that Martin won that year: he also took home the Best Short Story prize for his futuristic religious allegory *The Way of Cross and Dragon* – a powerful tale that, with its medieval imagery and visions of empire-forging dragons, is another vital precursor to *A Song of Ice and Fire*.

On a personal level, however, the 1970s would be less of a steady climb and more of a rollercoaster. Following the collapse of his 'great romance', Martin was married for the first time in 1975 to fellow sci-fi fan and convention organizer, Gale Burnick. When his stint with VISTA ended the following year, the newlyweds left Chicago for Dubuque, Iowa, where Martin had been offered a job teaching print journalism, composition and – to his delight – science-fiction literature at the local Clarke College. But his naive hope that full-time teaching would leave him plenty of time to write would be swiftly dashed: with 'lessons to be prepared, lectures to be written, papers to read, tests to grade, committees to attend, textbooks to review, students to counsel',[14]

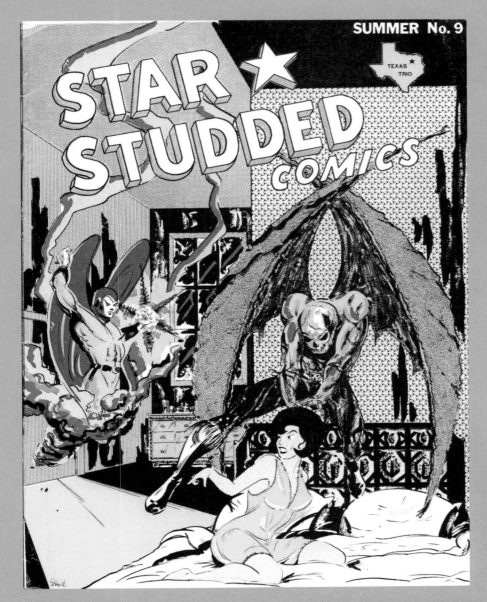

**TOP LEFT**
Pulp fiction: Issue #9 of *Star Studded Comics*, a fanzine that printed several early GRRM stories

**TOP RIGHT**
Peace and love: anti-war demonstrators gather around Chicago's Logan monument, August 1968

**BOTTOM RIGHT**
Have a cigar: author and editor Ben Bova signs for a young fan in 1967

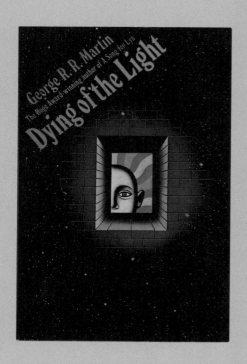

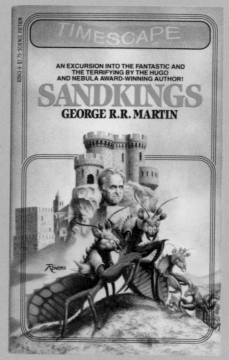

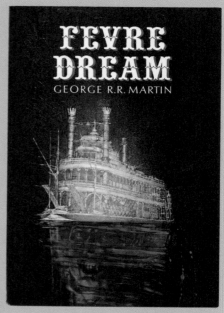

The early years: first edition covers of *Dying of the Light* (top left), *The Armageddon Rag* (top right) and *Fevre Dream* (bottom right), alongside short story collections *A Song For Lya* (top middle) and *Sandkings* (bottom left)

# 'Every man should lose a battle in his youth, so he does not lose a war when he is old'

Victarion Greyjoy, *A Feast for Crows*[15]

not to mention conventions, awards ceremonies and editorial work on a series of multi-author story collections entitled *New Voices* (1977–87), Martin's productivity once again began to dwindle.

Then, in 1979, the death of friend and fellow author, Tom Reamy, left Martin shaken. 'Do I have all the time in the world?' he would recall asking himself. 'I want to write all these stories.'[16] Finally biting the bullet, Martin quit his job to try and make it as a full-time writer. At the same time, he and Burnick decided they needed to make a move: though they had no local friends – just a passing acquaintance with SF legend Roger Zelazny – the pair had been sufficiently charmed on a brief visit to the city of Santa Fe, New Mexico that they decided to buy a home there. Sadly, however, 'the stress of separation, relocation, and a change in career proved too much for our marriage',[17] and the pair were soon divorced. Martin would remain in the city, however, and it wouldn't be long before his broken heart was well and truly healed.

The 1980s were another furiously busy decade for George R.R. Martin. His second novel, 1982's atmospheric deep-South vampire tale, *Fevre Dream*, was a solid seller, but the same could not be said of its successor, 1983's 'stereophonic long-playing novel' *The Armageddon Rag*.

Perhaps too steeped in the iconography of hippie-era psychedelic rock to appeal to a shiny, new-wave Reaganite audience, this fantasy-tinged mystery would be Martin's first flop and his last published novel for 13 years (his 1986 fix-up novel *Tuf Voyaging* is viewed by its author as a collection of short stories,[18] albeit with the same central character: space trader Haviland Tuf).

But *The Armageddon Rag* would find a small cadre of hardcore fans, and one of them happened to be a respected TV executive. Phil DeGuere's efforts to produce a film of Martin's novel would meet with a stony reception from the studios, but, in 1985, when he began collaborating with the CBS network on a reboot of the classic mystery show *The Twilight Zone*, DeGuere found himself able to offer Martin a job. Despite never having written for television before – and after being raised on horror stories of authors having their creative juices squeezed dry by the Hollywood machine – Martin nevertheless accepted, working on several episodes, including an adaptation of his friend Zelazny's *The Last Defender of Camelot* (published 1979, broadcast 1986). The show would falter after two seasons, but Martin's time in Tinseltown was only beginning. His home may have been Santa Fe, but between 1986 and 1992 Martin would spend much of his time

in Los Angeles, California, serving as a writer and supervising producer on CBS's dark fairy tale, *Beauty and the Beast* (1987–90), before pitching his own sci-fi show, *Doorways*, which got as far as the pilot stage in 1992 but never made it to a full series.

By this time, however, Martin had another ace up his sleeve – and another love in his life. The author had first encountered Parris McBride back in 1975, before his marriage to Gale Burnick; they'd kept in touch as friends, then in the early 1980s their romance was rekindled. McBride moved out to Santa Fe and, although it took 30 years to make things official – they were married in a small ceremony in 2011 – the couple have been together ever since.

It was McBride who first persuaded Martin to try his hand at role-playing games – a practice that, surprisingly, he'd never previously indulged in. Joining a local gaming group, many of whom were authors themselves, Martin and McBride became habitual players of *SuperWorld*, a superhero game that, as Martin writes, 'rekindled the frustrated comic book writer inside me'.[19]

As he and his fellow gamers honed their heroic characters and dispatched them on ever more complex adventures, the idea began to emerge of a shared-world anthology: a compilation of interlocking stories by different writers, all set within the same alternate universe where an alien virus has caused much of Earth's population to mutate and develop superhuman abilities. The result would be *Wild Cards*, a series of mosaic novels, edited initially by Martin and later by his friend and collaborator Melinda M. Snodgrass, first published in 1987 and now running to over 30 volumes.

For a number of years, it looked as if *Wild Cards* would be George R.R. Martin's lasting contribution to popular culture: the series has legions of fans worldwide and is still going strong. But then, in 1991, Martin had a vision. Three chapters into his first new novel in almost a decade, a sci-fi epic to be entitled *Avalon*, he was gripped by an idea that had nothing to do with the book he was writing. 'When I began, I didn't know

**On** September 27, 1986, a frustrated and angry impersonator is going to meet his idol...ELVIS! Join him as he crosses over...into The Twilight Zone.

**Season Premiere! New Night & Time!**

**The Twilight Zone**

**10PM CBS◉2**

**TOP LEFT**
Dealer's choice: the first book in the ongoing *Wild Cards* series of linked superhero stories

**TOP RIGHT**
Melinda Snodgrass, GRRM's long-time friend and close collaborator, pictured in 2012

**BOTTOM RIGHT**
Mad king: 1986 TV Guide ad for *The Twilight Zone* episode 'The Once and Future King', scripted by GRRM

**OPPOSITE**
Ours is the furry: a promotional image for *Beauty and the Beast* starring Linda Hamilton and Ron Perlman

# 'IDEAS ARE CHEAP ...
# IT'S THE EXECUTION
# THAT IS ALL-IMPORTANT'

George R.R. Martin[20]

# 'THE ODD THING ABOUT BEING A WRITER IS YOU DO TEND TO LOSE YOURSELF IN YOUR BOOKS'

George R.R. Martin[21]

what the hell I had,' he would say of the initial idea that would become the opening of *A Game of Thrones*. 'I thought it might be a short story; it was just this chapter, where they find these direwolf pups ... It was all there in my head, I couldn't not write it. So, it wasn't an entirely rational decision, but writers aren't entirely rational creatures.'[22]

From the beginning, Martin knew the tone that he wanted his new story to have. 'I thought these books could have the gritty feel of historical fiction, as well as some of the magic and awe of epic fantasy.' He also knew he was writing a trilogy – 'everybody was doing trilogies back then'[23] – so he wrote up the first 13 chapters and sent them to his agent, along with a rough three-page summary of the action to come.

However, this summary, which can be read online, differs wildly from the story we're familiar with, and rarely in a good way. In this version, Daenerys kills Khal Drogo in revenge for her brother; Sansa bears a child by Joffrey; and Jaime Lannister takes the throne of Westeros by 'killing everyone ahead of him in the line of succession and blaming his brother Tyrion for the murders'. Tyrion, meanwhile, falls 'helplessly in love with Arya Stark', setting the stage for 'a deadly rivalry between Tyrion and Jon Snow'.[24] Still, publishers were enthusiastic:

Martin received four offers, chose the best one, and started writing in earnest.

The world we encounter in *A Song of Ice and Fire* is so vivid and detailed, it's surprising to discover that, to a large extent, Martin simply made it up as he went along. 'I don't build the world first, then write in it. I just write the story, and then put it together ... You fill in a few things, then as you write more it becomes more and more alive.'[25] Of course, this simply serves to illustrate the primary position of storytelling in Martin's work: the plot and the characters take precedence, and everything else fits around them.

But it wasn't long before the plot started to get a bit out of control. 'By '95 I realized it had to be more than a trilogy,' Martin recalled later. 'Because I had 1,500 pages of manuscript (and) I wasn't anywhere close to the end of the first book. So, I said ... "I'm gonna have to break this first book into two books to get it all done."' He would also end up with many more characters than he'd anticipated. 'I have the biggest cast in literature,'[26] he admits proudly.

This huge spread of characters – every one of whom is meticulously listed in the back of each volume – may daunt new readers, but Martin's justification is simple. 'To present a complicated situation, you can't just tell

it all from the viewpoint of one person,' he told the *Austin Chronicle,* likening the scope of his books to an historical conflict like the First World War:

Is there one person who is absolutely central to WWI? No, you need ... someone on the eastern front, someone on the western front ... maybe a pacifist who's opposed to the war, or a communist ... then you need the Tsar or the King of England or the Prime Minister ... a wide variety of people. That was the number of people necessary to tell this story in all of its grandeur.[27]

And it was that very grandeur – that sprawling, breathtaking sense of scale – that would pull in readers from the beginning. Published in 1996, *A Game of Thrones* may not have been an out-of-the-gate bestseller, but it was a critical success: the *Chicago Sun-Times*, among others, praised the book's 'absorbing combination of the mythic, the sweepingly historical, and the intensely personal'.[28] It would go on to win the Locus award for Best Fantasy Novel, alongside a Hugo award for a novella entitled *Blood of the Dragon*, published in *Asimov's Science Fiction* magazine and comprising the Daenerys chapters from *A Game of Thrones*.

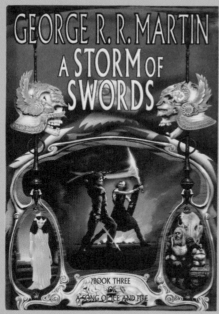

**TOP**
Man the battlements:
George R.R. Martin on the
*Game of Thrones* set in 2011

**BOTTOM LEFT**
The 2000 edition of the
third *A Song of Ice and Fire*
novel, *A Storm of Swords*

**BOTTOM RIGHT**
A wizard with words: the
1979 single-volume edition
of J.R.R. Tolkien's *The Lord
of the Rings*

The second volume, *A Clash of Kings*, would arrive in short order, reaching bookshelves in 1998 – it must have helped that around 300 pages had been lifted out of the previous volume. Again, reviews were glowing – 'easily as good as the first novel,' gushed *The Oregonian*, before warning readers that the level of sex and violence would make it wholly unsuitable 'for your 10-year-old nephew who likes Conan'.[29] Again, the book would win the Locus prize, an award also granted to the third volume, 2000's *A Storm of Swords* – a novel so vast that in many territories it would be published as two, three or even four separate books. This third instalment would be the first in the series to be nominated for a Hugo award for Best Novel, which it lost to *Harry Potter and the Goblet of Fire* – an absurd decision that seems even more so in retrospect. 'I would have liked to win that award and I don't think (J.K.) Rowling cares much about it,' Martin complained to an interviewer in 2012. 'And she didn't send anyone to accept the award, which is certainly annoying.'[30]

It was around this time, however, that Martin hit a snag. Regarding *A Storm of Swords* as the climax to an initial trilogy, with many key characters either dead or, like Arya and Daenerys, in a relatively settled position, the author began to look ahead to the second half of what was by then envisioned to be a six-book series. Set five years later, the first of these would cover Daenerys's invasion of Westeros, Jon Snow's encounters with the Others and Cersei's determination to cling to the Iron Throne. It was not to be.

What I soon discovered ... [was that the five-year gap] worked well with some characters ... [but with] other characters, it didn't work at all. Jon Snow ... at the end of *Storm* he gets elected Lord Commander. I'm picking up there, and writing 'Well, five years ago, I was elected Lord Commander. Nothing much has happened since then, but now things are starting to happen again.' Finally, after a year, I said, 'I can't make this work.'[31]

His solution was to write a bridging novel to span the intervening five years, introducing new locations like Dorne and the Iron Islands, while moving the established characters just far enough along to match the intended next volume. But again, things didn't go to plan: the book that would become *A Feast for Crows* was soon even longer than its predecessor, and this time Martin refused to split it down the middle. Instead, he opted to divide the book by storyline, lifting out some plot threads and moving them into a second book. The first of these volumes would arrive in 2005, but it would take another six years to complete the second: *A Dance With Dragons*, the fifth volume in what was now a planned seven-book epic, would emerge in 2011, by which time everything would be very different in the world of George R.R. Martin.

We'll explore HBO's *Game of Thrones* – its production, its impact and its relationship to its source novels – in more detail in the epilogue to this volume. For now, suffice it to say that the immense popularity of the show – and Martin's own involvement in the writing, pre-production and marketing of both that series and its 2022 spin-off, *House of the Dragon* – served not only to limit his writing time, but to pile the immense pressure of expectation on the next volume in the series. Martin himself has expressed regret about the length of time it takes him to produce new books – 'Why did I ever tackle such a big project?' he'd moan, half-jokingly, in 2013. 'Did it really have to be seven kingdoms? Couldn't it have been five kingdoms? Five is a good number!'[32]

But the truth is that George R.R. Martin is attempting a writing project on a scale unrivalled by just about any other composition since the Bible. At 1,770,000 words, *A Song of Ice and Fire* is already more than three times the length of Martin's beloved *The Lord of the Rings* by J.R.R. Tolkien (1954–55); it's also half a million words longer than the entirety of Proust's *A La Recherche du Temps Perdu* (*In Search of Lost Time*; 1913–27), and rather more fun to read. Longer-running fantasy series do exist –

Raymond E. Feist's Riftwar cycle (1982–2013) stands at 30 books, while Piers Anthony's Xanth books (1977–present) number an extraordinary 45 – but few of these have the breadth and intricacy of Martin's creation, the huge spread of interlocking narratives and the sheer diversity of characters.

So how did a writer best known for short stories come to craft such a gigantic sequence of novels? What sources – historical, literary and personal – did he draw upon in the writing, and what inspiration did they give him? These are some of the questions this work of criticism and review will seek to answer – with one small caveat. The sheer breadth of George R.R. Martin's influences means that if I was to cover everything, there would be far too much material to fit into a single volume – and, unlike the maestro, I'm not about to spin this book off into a multi-part series. So, if you discover that a favourite source isn't mentioned or that a particular theory you might've encountered on one of the many discussion forums and blogs dedicated to the worlds of Westeros isn't included, please put it down to restrictions of length, rather than ignorance.

Now, without further prevarication, let us take our first step into the world of Ice and Fire, beginning at the extreme end of the known world: that vast structure that stands as a bulwark against the forces of darkness.

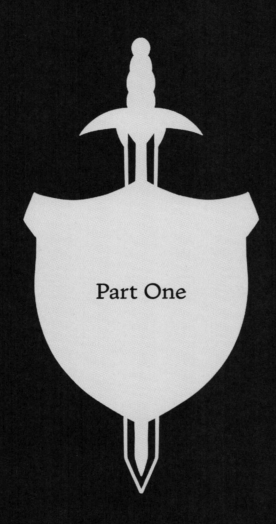

Part One

# THE
# NORTH

Chapter One

# THE WALL

In 1981, following the collapse of his first marriage, George R.R. Martin left America for the first time, travelling to England to visit his ex-partner and fellow author, Lisa Tuttle, with whom he'd collaborated on a trio of stories that had just been published as the fix-up novel *Windhaven*. Touring the country and visiting many of its most ancient sights, the pair made a stop at Hadrian's Wall, the man-made fortification that had once marked the border between the 'civilized' Roman Empire and the 'barbaric' wilderness beyond. 'I remember it was the end of the day, near sunset,' Martin would recall. 'The tour buses were leaving … it was fall and the wind was blowing. I tried to imagine how it would be (for) a Roman legionary … That wall was the edge of the known world, protecting their cities from the enemies behind the wall. I experienced a lot of feelings there, looking to the North.'[1]

Running 120 km (73 miles) west-to-east, from the shores of the Solway Firth – a coastal inlet that still forms part of the border between England and Scotland – to the fort of Segedunum in what is now Tyneside, Hadrian's Wall is one of the marvels of Roman construction. Standing at least 2.5 m (8 ft) wide and 3.5 m (12 ft) high – though it may initially have stood taller – the wall was lined with small fortifications or 'milecastles' with two watchtowers between each one, plus full-size forts spaced roughly 11 km (7 miles) apart. There were also ditches on either side and regular pits or *cippi* spiked with sharpened branches to further deter the Scots raiders who came to steal cattle, belongings and even slaves. Begun in AD 122 under the reign of the emperor Hadrian, the wall would take more than six years to complete and employ some 15,000 Roman troops as builders and stonemasons. Initially comprising as many as 10,000 men, the garrison would dwindle in later years as the empire itself faded.

Of course, the physical dimensions of Hadrian's Wall may seem minuscule in comparison with the Wall of Westeros, which stands a somewhat more impressive 480 km (300 miles) long, 210 m (700 ft) high and 90 m (300 ft) wide, marking an impassable barrier across the entire continent. But Hadrian's Wall served a different purpose from Martin's in one vital respect: it wasn't built to keep the Scots out, only to slow them down. Because it wasn't only raiders who wanted to enter the province of Britannia. Traders and farmers also made the crossing, and these were a key part of the local economy – cutting them off would have done more harm than good. According to historians, the purpose of the wall was to give the Romans control over the border, and the ability to turn back undesirables. Of course, it also worked to hinder the passage of any raiding parties, giving time to raise the alarm and call for reinforcements.

However, recent research suggests there may be one significant similarity between the two great walls. In *A Game of Thrones*, Martin describes Jon Snow's first encounter with the Wall: 'a pale blue line across the northern horizon … vanishing into the far distance, immense and unbroken.' At Castle Black, he learns that the Wall has many moods: 'It often seemed a pale grey, the colour of an overcast sky … but when the sun caught it fair on a bright day, it *shone*, alive with light.'[2] Likewise, the Roman wall may have been more than just a dull stone barrier. 'There is some evidence that Hadrian's Wall was covered in plaster and then whitewashed,' claims the website *English History*, 'which would have meant it would have reflected the sunlight and been visible for miles around.'[3]

In both cases, then, these walls would act not just as a physical barrier, but a psychological one. For the people of Westeros – Wildlings and Night's Watch alike – the Wall marks a clear line between the relative security and refinement of the Seven Kingdoms and the lawless wilderness

A land divided: the Wall of Westeros as seen in *Game of Thrones* (top), and its real-world inspiration, Hadrian's Wall (bottom)

'History is a wheel, for the nature of man is fundamentally unchanging. What has happened before will perforce happen again.'

Archmaester Rigney, *A Feast for Crows*[4]

beyond. And Hadrian's Wall would have played a similar role, letting those coming from the north know that once they stepped across the border, they would enter a different world with different customs and laws – a world where the Romans had the power. As historian Jarrett A. Lobell puts it: 'until the end of Roman rule in Britain ... Hadrian's Wall was the clearest statement possible of the might, resourcefulness, and determination of an individual emperor and of his empire.'[5]

The Wall is the first great location that we learn of in *A Game of Thrones*; it's mentioned during the prologue, in the very first handful of pages. Soon we'll encounter the Others – renamed the White Walkers in the TV adaptation, perhaps to avoid confusion with the recently concluded mystery show *Lost* (2004–2010) – a race of ruthless killers whose ice-blue eyes clearly mark them out as a supernatural threat. But before any of that, we'll meet three characters who could have stepped straight from the pages of a medieval history book: a knight, a poacher and a faithful retainer, all of them bickering and griping as they go about their duties.

Thus, from the outset, *A Song of Ice and Fire* marks itself out as a blend of genres – what its author would describe as 'a hybrid... inspired as much by the historical fiction of Thomas B. Costain and Nigel

Tranter as the fantasy of Tolkien, [Robert E.] Howard and Fritz Leiber.'[6] We'll return to Martin's relationship with fantasy literature later in this volume (see page 95), but first let's explore perhaps the most significant influence on the entire series, and the one that separates *A Song of Ice and Fire* from the vast majority of its fantastical predecessors: historical fiction.

George R.R. Martin's love of historical literature is not confined to the two names listed above, both of whom penned romantic adventure stories set in medieval times. For the Canadian journalist-turned-author Costain, his most successful book was 1945's *The Black Rose*, about a young Saxon clerk who sets off to the far-flung kingdom of Cathay – the medieval name for China – encountering numerous historical figures along the way. The wildly prolific, Glasgow-born Tranter, meanwhile, kept his focus firmly on his homeland, publishing works of both fiction and non-fiction following the exploits of Robert the Bruce, King James V, Mary Queen of Scots and others. Their names may be relatively obscure today, but in their heyday – the 1940s and 1950s for Costain, the 1960s, 1970s and 1980s for Tranter – both writers were enormously popular on both sides of the Atlantic.

Other historical novels cited by Martin include Sir Arthur Conan Doyle's *The White Company* (1891), which provided

**TOP LEFT**
Medieval adventurer: Canadian journalist and historical fiction writer Thomas B. Costain

**BOTTOM AND TOP RIGHT**
George R.R. Martin with his former paramour and writing partner Lisa Tuttle, and (above) the 1981 first edition of their 'fix-up' novel, *Windhaven*

# 'Many good men have been bad kings ... and some bad men have been good kings'

Archmaester Rigney, *A Feast for Crows*[7]

inspiration for the Free Companies of Essos; Sir Walter Scott's *Ivanhoe* (1819), one of the key texts concerning chivalric heroism; and Charles Dickens's *A Tale of Two Cities*, published in 1859 but set almost a century earlier, during the French Revolution, and selected by Martin as one of his five favourite novels in any genre when asked by the New York Public Library.[8]

Among contemporary authors, he's an avowed fan of British-born bestseller-list staple, Bernard Cornwell – 'no one writes better historical fiction',[9] according to Martin – and of American author Diana Gabaldon, whose time-travelling *Outlander* series (1991–present) also combines historical fiction with a fantasy element. On his 'Not a Blog', Martin goes even further, offering readers an exhaustive list of approved historical authors including 'Howard Pyle, Frank Yerby, Rosemary Hawley Jarman ... George McDonald Fraser ... Sharon Kay Penman, Steven Pressfield, Cecelia Holland, David Anthony Durham [and] David Ball.'[10]

But the author he would call 'my hero'[11] was a Frenchman: playwright, novelist, scholar, Resistance fighter and recipient of the *Ordre national de la Légion d'honneur*, the *Ordre des Arts et des Lettres* and the Order of the British Empire, Maurice Druon. Published between 1955 and 1977, Druon's seven-book series *Les Rois maudits*, or *The Accursed Kings*, takes place in the fourteenth century and follows the fortunes of seven French rulers in the years preceding the outbreak of the Hundred Years War between France and England. Describing them as 'the original game of thrones',[12] Martin

was instrumental in publisher Harper Collins's decision to reprint the series in 2013. *The Accursed Kings* has it all,' he would write at the time. 'Iron kings and strangled queens, battles and betrayals, lies and lust, deception, family rivalries ... the doom of a great dynasty and all of it (or most of it) straight from the pages of history.'[13]

The 'great dynasty' of Druon's series were the Capetians, who – like the Targaryen family in *A Song of Ice and Fire* – had ruled in an unbroken line for centuries, only to be replaced in 1328 by the House of Valois. Like Westeros, France was made up of separate feudal states all paying homage to a single king, so the downfall of the Capetian dynasty would have affected every part of the realm. And there are specific character parallels, too, like the powerful princess Isabella, known as the She-Wolf of France and later to become Queen of England, who clearly informs the ambitious and deadly Cersei Lannister. Indeed, in her essay on the subject, medievalist Professor Carolyne Larrington identifies at least five points of strong comparison between Druon's work and Martin's, from the regular use of poison and the central role of bankers in the narrative to the tiny cell in which Edward II is imprisoned, which opens onto a deep well and slopes downwards, just like poor Tyrion Lannister's dungeon at The Eyrie. 'Martin learned a great deal from Druon in terms of managing a complex interweaving of personal narratives,' she writes, 'and in setting out large-scale historical changes and political conspiracies.'[14]

But, as mentioned earlier, while he may borrow from such sources, Martin has no interest in simply rewriting history (or indeed historical fiction), with added dragons. As he told Bernard Cornwell when the two authors sat down together in 2012: 'Fantasists enjoy certain freedoms that historical novelists do not. I can surprise my readers by killing kings and other major characters, but ... in the real world ... we know who lives and who dies before we ever crack the novel open.'[15] That said, he does prefer to take much of his inspiration from relatively obscure

Tip of the hat: GRRM has acknowledged his debt to Maurice Druon, pictured here during his time as France's Culture Minister, alongside his wife, Madeleine

# 'HISTORY IS WRITTEN IN BLOOD'

George R.R. Martin[16]

historical incidents: while we may all be familiar with Hadrian's Wall and the Norman Conquest, how many of us are schooled enough to spot references to the Tour de Nesle affair in fourteenth-century France, or the Black Dinner of 1440? This fictionalization also gives Martin license to pick and choose historical periods to suit the story he's telling, so while the Wall may have its roots in the Classical period, much of *A Song of Ice and Fire* is drawn from medieval history or even later, with references to the trial of Anne Boleyn and locations that would seem to be drawn straight from Dickens.

For Martin, the outcome of all this has been unexpectedly delightful. 'I find it amusing, and secretly pleasing, that I have so many fans who are interested in the history (of Westeros),' he says. 'Perhaps they're bored with all the Henrys in English history, but they'll gladly follow the Targaryen dynasty. History is ... a gold mine – the kings, the princes, the generals and the whores, and all the betrayals and wars and confidences. It's better than 90 per cent of what the fantasists do make up.'[17]

It's also much bloodier, which is another part of the appeal. 'There's something very close up about the Middle Ages', Martin enthuses. 'You're taking a sharp piece of steel and hacking at someone's head, and you're getting spattered with his blood, and you're hearing his screams.' Accusations that *A Song of Ice and Fire* is overly brutal, or too concerned with violence, hold no sway with the author. 'Yes, Westeros is a violent and cruel world, but no more so than the real Middle Ages. In some ways, Westeros is Disneyland compared to some of the things that really went on during the Crusades or the Hundred Years War.'[18]

This sense of brutal realism also provides a clear dividing line between *A Game of Thrones* and its most obvious literary ancestors, the works of J.R.R. Tolkien and his imitators. '*Lord of the Rings* had a very medieval philosophy: that if the king was a good man, the land would prosper,' Martin says. 'We look at real history and it's not that simple ... What was Aragorn's tax policy? Did he maintain a standing army? What did he do in times of flood and famine? And what about all these orcs ... Did Aragorn pursue a policy of systematic genocide and kill them? Even the little baby orcs, in their little orc cradles?'[19]

It is at the Wall that moral questions such as these will become particularly pressing. At the outset, the situation there seems simple. On one side are the Night's Watch, the 'shield that guards the realms

Mounted knights clash at the Battle of Las Navas de Tolosa in Spain, in the year 1212

of men',[20] a band of brothers with their roots in medieval orders of chivalry, like the Knights Templar, who banded together to protect pilgrims making the journey to the Holy Land, and who, like the Night's Watch, took vows of chastity and poverty. On the other are the Wildlings: barbarian tribes known to raid Northern villages, slaughtering men and carrying off cattle, women and children. Their inspiration goes back to the time of Hadrian and the tribes of Scots who marauded along the border, known to the Romans as Picts, though this may have been a pejorative term.

But in Westeros, just as in real life, nothing is as straightforward as it seems. The Night's Watch aren't a noble fraternity, but a dwindling, increasingly desperate band of exiles and criminals: 'a midden heap for all the misfits of the realm',[21] as Tyrion Lannister tells the horrified Jon Snow. And the Wildlings aren't simple marauders, either: like the tribes of ancient Scotland, they have unique cultural identities, fromthe organized and warlike Thenns tothe cannibalistic Ice-River Clans. Due to a lack of written history, it's hard to say exactly how many different Pictish tribes there were, but one remaining source, an ancient Irish poem known as *Seven Children of Cruithne*, actually identifies the same number of

Pictish realms as there are kingdoms in Westeros, each one established by one of the seven sons of Cruithne, the mythical founder of the Pictish people. Whatever the reality, the Pictish peoples certainly had a number of separate ruling dynasties – some of them matriarchal, and each with their own traditions, including extraordinary artworks made from stone, bone and silver.

By *A Storm of Swords*, we've become aware that, although the Wildlings may have an army poised to enter the Seven Kingdoms, they are, in fact, fleeing for their lives, not seeking conquest. We might even detect a rare hint of allegory in Martin's writing here, as these Wildling refugees gamble with their very lives in a desperate bid for security, just like the men and women who cross America's heavily militarized southern border every day, or those brave souls who risk the stormy waters of the Mediterranean and the English Channel (we even hear of Wildlings forced to 'cross the Bay of Seals in little boats'[22]). And it's also one of the few times Martin offers his readers something akin to hope, as first Stannis Baratheon and then Jon Snow offer the Wildlings sanctuary south of the Wall, provided they'll help the Night's Watch defend it against their common enemy: the Others.

'THEY WERE COLD THINGS, DEAD THINGS, THAT HATED IRON AND FIRE AND THE TOUCH OF THE SUN, AND EVERY CREATURE WITH HOT BLOOD IN ITS VEINS'

Old Nan, *A Game of Thrones*[23]

The lives of others: the terrifying White Walkers from *Game of Thrones*, as played by Ross Mullan (top) and Vladimir Furdik (bottom)

In an email to artist Tommy Patterson during their collaboration on a *Game of Thrones* graphic novel, Martin compared the Others to ancient Irish myths of the *Sidhe* or *Aos sí*, capricious and powerful mythic beings to whom offerings must be given. 'The Others are not dead,' he wrote. 'They are strange, beautiful ... think of *Sidhe* made of ice ... a different sort of life ... inhuman, elegant, dangerous.'[24] Appearing in many Gaelic legends and folk tales and possessed of numerous names, including *Dhaoine Uaisle* or the Noble Folk and *Slúagh na Marbh* or Host of the Dead, the *Sidhe* are intimately connected to the Irish landscape, and committed to defending their sacred places. And though it is not yet clear in the books precisely what the ultimate objective of the Others will prove to be, the defence of the natural world from human invasion would seem to be a factor.[25]

Their shambling corpse-slaves, known as wights, also have a medieval precedent: the Norse *draugr,* undead beings who jealously guarded their burial mounds from any who would seek to steal their treasure, and whose bodies often needed to be burned before they could take their final rest. It was, however, easier to outwit a *draug* than to destroy one of Martin's wights: as Professor Larrington writes in her book *Winter is Coming,* about the medieval history underpinning *Game of Thrones,* if the corpse is first decapitated, and 'his head is placed ... behind him with the face against the buttocks, he becomes confused and does not revive'.[26] Men of the Watch, take note!

Of course, the word wight also crops up in *The Lord of the Rings*: in a scene presumably inspired by medieval scholar Tolkien's own knowledge of the *draugr* myth, our Hobbit heroes become lost among the ancient gravesites of the Barrow-downs and wake up under attack from undead creatures. And the Others, too, might have a dash of Tolkien in their DNA: spectral figures on horseback who wield cursed blades and know no fear, they are every bit as otherworldly as the Nazgul, or Black Riders, in Tolkien's novel.

But it's a different kind of fiction that most informs these supernatural killers.

Martin's relationship with horror fiction goes right back to childhood, and the monster movies he'd catch at Bayonne's Victory cinema or on TV, often featuring Dracula, The Wolf Man or Frankenstein ('he was always Frankenstein to us, never ... "the monster"'[27]). And he had written several scary stories in the years before *A Song of Ice and Fire* – notably his second novel, *Fevre Dream* (1982); his 1980 sci-fi/horror hybrid novella *Nightflyers* (the first of Martin's works to be adapted into a movie, though not a very good one); and 1988's contemporary werewolf tale *The Skin Trade*.

Later, he would discover the work of H.P. Lovecraft, whose visions of uncanny creatures from outside of time and space would be yet another clear influence on the implacable, relentless Others. Lovecraft's tales of remote, abandoned cities would also feed into *A Clash of Kings*, as Daenerys Targaryen and her shrinking khalasar stumble upon a lost desert metropolis that they name Vaes Tolorro, or 'city of bones'. 'When I need a scary effect in a book [that I'm writing],' Martin would tell an audience in 2017, 'I reach for Lovecraft.'[28]

Almost a century after his death in 1937, Howard Phillips Lovecraft remains one of the most controversial figures in American literature. The creator of some 60-plus tales of irrational dread and eldritch horror – most notably those that make up his nebulous and inexplicable Cthulhu Mythos, with its visions of vast, ancient creatures seeking to enter our own reality – he was also for much of his life a committed white supremacist who frequently disparaged people of other races. His legacy, then, is a complex one: while his stories are still hugely influential on every writer of horror fiction – and most authors of fantasy, too – Lovecraft's work is constantly being reappraised and reinterpreted, notably by the 2016 novel *Lovecraft Country* by Matt Ruff and its 2020 TV adaptation, which smartly used Lovecraftian imagery to explore issues of race and segregation in 1950s America.

In 1986, George R.R. Martin served as the editor of a horror compendium entitled *Night Visions 3,* in whose

introduction he writes: 'A good horror story will frighten us, yes. It will keep us awake at night, it will make our flesh crawl ... [But] the best horror stories are stories first and horror second ... They concern themselves not simply with fear, but with life in all its infinite variety.'[29] As always, it is the story and the characters that, for Martin, claim the highest priority.

**TOP LEFT**
This 1936 issue of *Astounding Stories* featured the first appearance of H.P. Lovecraft's icebound classic *At the Mountains of Madness*

**TOP RIGHT**
The ancient one: a sketch of the great god Cthulhu by H.P. Lovecraft

**BOTTOM**
B-movie battle: Lon Chaney and Bela Lugosi go mano a monster in 1943's *Frankenstein vs The Wolf Man*

**OVERLEAF**
Forces of nature: the 1911 artwork *Riders of the Sidhe* by John Duncan

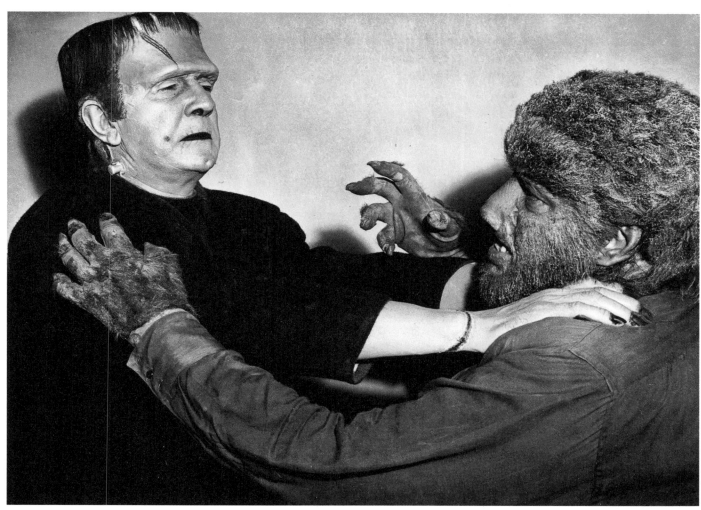

Chapter Two

# WINTERFELL

As central to events in *A Song of Ice and Fire* as the Wall itself, the castle of Winterfell is the seat of power in the Northern kingdom and the ancestral home of the Stark family. Built close to the Kingsroad that runs like a spine from north to south, Winterfell is ringed by two concentric shield walls with a moat between them and is large enough to encompass a number of fortified keeps and towers, a feasting hall, a glass-covered garden and a godswood centred around a mighty weirwood tree. Constructed over a natural hot spring, the castle has warm water piped through the walls of its bedchambers, ensuring that its inhabitants remain comfortable, even in the depths of the Northern winter.

This idea of natural central heating may be Roman in origin – the use of underground springs or *thermae* to heat buildings was widely used, notably in Pompeii and the English city of Bath – but everything else about Winterfell is staunchly medieval. From the heart of the Great Keep to its mighty outer defences, the castle contains countless echoes of those fortifications built across Europe, but particularly in Britain, from around the twelfth to the sixteenth centuries.

While George R.R. Martin has never named any specific British castle as inspiration, we know that he has visited several, both on his trip with Lisa Tuttle and in the years since, so it's safe to assume that these visits would feed into his creation of Winterfell and the many other strongholds of Westeros. Often constructed on the ruins of Roman buildings or on raised ramparts of rock and earth, these castles often started out as a simple wood or stone palisade called a motte-and-bailey. They were then expanded and fortified over the years or even centuries, with outer towers and curtain walls added to the existing structure, so that anyone attacking would have to surmount several layers of defence before reaching the central keep.

Again, such castles weren't built purely for military or defensive purposes: like Hadrian's Wall, they would also have had a powerful psychological objective, acting as conspicuous statements of power and privilege that dominated whatever landscape they were built into. One particularly striking example is Harlech Castle in North Wales, built by Edward I of England during his invasion of that country in the thirteenth century as a statement of English dominance over the rebellious Welsh (more of whom later in this volume, see page 134). Built upon a huge spur of rock overlooking the sea, the castle utilizes concentric walls and features a gatehouse with three portcullises and two heavy doors. It would play a key role in the fifteenth-century Wars of the Roses, where it was held by Lancastrian forces against King Edward IV and his Yorkist allies.

Other existing castles that might have inspired the great keeps of Westeros are Arundel Castle in Sussex, whose notoriety for being 'cold, dark and unfriendly'[1] would seem to prefigure the monstrous stronghold of Harrenhal with its 'cavernous halls and ruined towers ... ruinous to heat, impossible to garrison';[2] and the enormous Dover Castle in Kent, which, like the Red Keep of King's Landing, occupies a key position on the coast. Built to repel invaders from the sea, Dover is said to be the largest castle in England, though this claim is also made by the eleventh-century royal residence of Windsor Castle.

Yet, however massive these castles are, they cannot rival the vast fortifications of Westeros. Depicted in the opening scenes of HBO's spin-off series *House of the Dragon*, the Great Council of 101AC, held to decide the Targaryen succession, was staged at Harrenhal because the organizers 'thought [it] prudent to have room for at least 500 lords and their tails',[3] while the Red Keep is described as having seven drum-towers, each with 3.5-m (12-ft) thick walls. Even Winterfell,

**LEFT**
An artist's rendering of a motte-and-bailey castle in Norman England

**RIGHT**
After the fall: the eighteenth-century artwork *Ruins of a Roman Bath With Washerwomen* by Hubert Robert

though smaller than many, has still been constructed on a scale unimaginable to medieval builders: 'a grey stone labyrinth of walls and towers and courtyards and tunnels spreading out in all directions ... like some monstrous stone tree.'[4]

Indeed, as young Bran Stark scales the great walls in search of 'the crows' nests atop the broken tower, where no one ever went but him',[5] we might be reminded not of a real-world castle but an imaginary one, dreamed up by another of George R.R. Martin's favourite writers. Like Winterfell, the castle of Gormenghast, created by the British author and illustrator Mervyn Peake in his 1946 novel *Titus Groan* and its sequels, is a sprawling warren of a place, with many more abandoned towers than occupied ones. And, like Winterfell, it has a committed climber, the Machiavellian anti-hero, Steerpike, who, like Bran, navigates the castle from above, clambering over 'the roofscape of Gormenghast, its crags and its stark walls of cliff pocked with nameless windows'.[6]

Martin's affection for Peake runs deep. Not only did he choose the Gormenghast trilogy as one of his favourite fantasy novels in a list of Reading Recommendations in 2013,[7] he even went so far as to name a character in the author's honour: Lord Titus Peake, husband of Lady Margot Lannister and Lord of the nudgingly named

Starpike. Again, we find Martin fusing real-life inspirations with imaginary ones, and coming up with something altogether his own.

When it comes to the family who occupy Winterfell, however, their real-life antecedents would seem glaringly obvious. The nominative similarity between the names of the Stark clan and their bitter rivals, the Lannisters, and the two families at the heart of the medieval Wars of the Roses – York and Lancaster – is perhaps the best-known of all the historical resonances in *A Song of Ice and Fire*, with even the author admitting that 'probably the main influence on *Ice and Fire* is the War [sic] of the Roses.'[8] He has even stated that 'I did consider at a very early stage ... writing a Wars of the Roses novel'.[9]

Waged between 1455 and 1487 and known at the time simply as the Civil Wars, the Wars of the Roses were a series of conflicts over the English succession between two wealthy branches of the Plantagenet family that had held the English throne since the accession of Henry II three centuries earlier. Both the duchies of York and Lancaster had solid claims to the throne, and indeed the war would only end when the two dynasties were finally united under the banner of the House of Tudor.

# 'ALL SORTS OF PEOPLE ARE CALLING THEMSELVES KINGS THESE DAYS'

Tyrion Lannister, *A Clash of Kings*[10]

So, how much does Martin's work really owe to this storied conflict? There are articles online claiming that *A Song of Ice and Fire* – or at least the War of Five Kings that begins in the first book and dominates the next two – maps closely onto its historical predecessor. They point to the enmity between the real-life Richard of York – an experienced military leader who attempted to rein in the excesses of the unworthy and often unstable King Henry VI – and the king's wife, Margaret of Anjou, who strived to claim her own stake in the rulership of the kingdom. Indeed, Margaret – an ambitious and talented woman who 'excelled all other, as well in beauty and favour, as in wit and policy, and was of stomach and courage, more like to a man, than a woman'[11] – has obvious parallels with another powerful queen, Cersei Lannister. Margaret even laid a trap for her enemy strikingly similar to the one that Cersei uses to ensnare Ned Stark, luring Richard of York to an apparently innocent meeting with the king before placing him under house arrest and forcing him to swear an oath of allegiance, much as Ned is driven to do on the steps of the Sept of Baelor.

But Richard did not lose his head for his efforts – at least, not immediately – and indeed, the differences between Richard of York and the head of the Stark family far outweigh the similarities. Richard was headstrong, power-hungry, ultimately willing to take the country to war in order to claim the crown for himself. Ned, meanwhile, is self-effacing and peaceable, worried for his friend King Robert and only driven to challenge Cersei when he feels he has no other choice. Other correspondences between reality and fiction do occur throughout the story – the sudden marriage of Ned's son Robb Stark to the daughter of a minor lord echoes the surprise wedding of Richard's son Edward IV to the relatively insignificant Elizabeth Woodville, while the character of Edward himself – a strapping, energetic warrior, always at the heart of the battle – must surely have fed into Ned's memories of the young Robert Baratheon.

But efforts to directly map other famous incidents from the medieval war – like the murder of the Princes in the Tower – onto Martin's work seem doomed to failure. Are the princes Bran and Rickon? Or the sons of Rhaegar Targaryen? Either way, it doesn't quite work.

The author himself dismisses talk of easy parallels. 'The Wars of the Roses have always fascinated me,' he said as far back as 1998, 'and certainly did influence *A Song of Ice and Fire*, but there's really no one-for-one character-for-character correspondence.'[12] As already noted, Cersei could just as easily be compared to Isabella as to Margaret of Anjou – both women were known at one time or another as the She-Wolf of France – while Westeros has much more in common with the jostling states of medieval France than it does with the relatively united England. As ever, Martin is willing to borrow from all over the historical map to feed the furnace of his imagination.

More than any specific incident or individual, what conflicts like the Wars of the Roses and the Hundred Years War give to *A Song of Ice and Fire* is a vision of medieval warfare as endless and brutal, waged by the expendable at the whim of the powerful. The battles in Martin's books may be diverse in location and technique, from the hectic and bloody Battle on the Green Fork to the bridge of burning boats at the Battle of the Blackwater. They may be viewed from a variety of perspectives: 'sometimes I employ the private's viewpoint, very up close and personal, dropping the reader right into the middle of the carnage,' Martin told Bernard Cornwell. 'Sometimes I go with the general's point of view instead, looking down from on high, seeing lines and flanks and reserves.'[13] But what all these battles share is that they reflect different aspects of medieval warfare, be it close-up melee combat with swords, battle-axes, clubs and spears; siege warfare against fortified castles, utilizing catapults, battering rams, trebuchets and towers; ranged warfare using crossbows, longbows and throwing spears; or mounted combat between armoured knights on horseback.

**LEFT**
Cersei's forebear? Margaret of Anjou with her husband King Henry VI, from the *Shrewsbury Talbot Book of Romances*, c. 1445

**RIGHT**
Dead or alive? The 1878 painting *The Princes in the Tower* by John Everett Millais

# 'STICK THEM WITH THE POINTY END'

Jon Snow, *A Game of Thrones*[14]

The bastard in battle:
Kit Harington as
the blood-soaked
Jon Snow in
*Game of Thrones*

'There is a savage beast in every man, and when you hand that man a sword or spear and send him forth to war, the beast stirs'

Ser Jorah Mormont, *A Storm of Swords*[15]

This latter fighting style was first employed in Europe during the early Middle Ages and utilized to great effect at the Battle of Hastings in 1066 by William the Conqueror, an obvious antecedent to Westeros's historical invader, Aegon the Conqueror. At Hastings, despite having the high-ground advantage, the English forces were routed, thanks in large part to William's possession of armoured cavalry. In Westeros, the equivalent battle was the Field of Fire, in which a much larger force was destroyed by Aegon and his sisters thanks to their possession of the ultimate military technology of the age – dragons.

At Hastings, the English forces would have been made up largely of serfs, sworn men in the service of their liege lords. These militias were unpaid and, in many cases, entirely inexperienced in the arts of war – in the incomplete Old English poem *The Battle of Maldon*, recounting a clash between Anglo-Saxon forces and Viking raiders, we read how Byrhtnoth, the Earl of Essex, 'marshalled his soldiers, riding and instructing, directing his warriors how they should stand and the positions they should keep'.[16] And though it's never explicitly spelled out, the suggestion is that the armed men of Westeros – those 'smallfolk' who do a large part of the fighting and the vast majority of the dying – are similarly unpaid, untrained and often poorly equipped.

By the time of the Hundred Years War, however, the soldiers on Europe's battlefields would by and large have been paid professionals, much like the sellswords who range throughout Westeros, offering their steel to any man who'll pay. In Italy, particularly, mercenary companies commanded high prices – but that's a topic we'll return to when we come to cover the Free Cities of Essos, later in this volume (see page 148).

Perhaps the most noticeable parallel between a real historical battle and a fictional one arrives towards the end of *A Clash of Kings*. The second siege of Constantinople predates the medieval period, beginning in AD 717, as Arab forces of the Umayyad Caliphate, under the command of the great general Maslama ibn Abd al-Malik, attempted to overrun the capital city of the Byzantine or eastern Roman Empire. Attacking both on land and in a great fleet of purpose-built ships at a time when the empire was riven by internal strife, the Arabs seemed to have the advantage. But as they approached the city walls, the defending army responded with a hail of 'Greek fire', a combustible substance whose exact recipe is now lost to history, but which probably included a combination of naphtha – extracted from crude oil – and quicklime.

**TOP**
Military might: a detail from the eleventh-century Bayeux tapestry shows English foot soldiers facing mounted French cavalry

**BOTTOM**
'The substance burns so hot it melts steel': Byzantine sailors deploy Greek fire against their Saracen enemies in this twelfth-century illustration

In *A Song of Ice and Fire*, the corresponding substance is known as wildfire, and it's used to destroy Stannis Baratheon's fleet as he approaches King's Landing at the Battle of the Blackwater. But the parallels don't end there: when the Arab fleet attempted to retreat from Constantinople through the natural estuary known as the Golden Horn, they found their way blocked by a huge chain, forcing them to move further inland, where they fell prey to the Byzantine forces. This exact trick is employed by Tyrion Lannister against Stannis's fleet, with much the same result: the siege fails and thousands lose their lives.

For George R.R. Martin, war is always a messy affair: it's bloody, vicious and often completely meaningless, and the scars it leaves behind are near impossible to heal. It's worth noting again that Martin was a conscientious objector during the Vietnam War and thus never saw combat, but he would nonetheless have been exposed to the war through news reports and articles, not to mention the first-hand accounts of returning soldiers. Tales of the massacres of civilian populations,

of villages burned and innocents put to death, were all widely reported by the American media during the late 1960s and early 1970s. Reading the Arya chapters in *A Clash of Kings* – in which she encounters just such horrors committed by both Lannister and Stark forces against the population of the Riverlands – it's impossible not to think of events like the My Lai massacre on 16 March 1968, just one of countless atrocities committed by both sides during that conflict. 'There's only a few wars that are really worth what they cost,' Martin would say in 2014. 'We're all capable of doing great things, and of doing bad things. We have the angels and the demons inside of us, and our lives are a succession of choices.'[17]

One of the few figures in the series who makes a concerted effort to avoid war, by agreeing to allow the Wildlings safe passage through the Wall, is, of course, the bastard Jon Snow. Though fans have made efforts to pair Jon up with historical or folkloric heroes, from Robert the Bruce to King Arthur, none are particularly convincing – but bastards were, unsurprisingly, commonplace throughout the medieval period, and many of them achieved remarkable things. Take the aforementioned William the Conqueror, born of an unwed couple and known for much of his life as William the Bastard, who went on to become the first Norman king of England.

It helped that, like another notorious bastard in *A Song of Ice and Fire*, William had three things in his favour: his father, known as Robert the Magnificent, was a major noble, the Duke of Normandy; that same father took the decision to publicly recognize his son before a council of his supporters; and he also left no other male heir to challenge William's legitimacy. In fact, William and Ramsay Snow – later Bolton – have a fair bit more in common: both are talented military strategists, and both are notoriously brutal. But while Ramsay may hunt, castrate and flay his victims alive, William's exploits were even more monstrous. Waged from the years 1069–70, his campaign of terror against the north of England – known as the Harrying of the North – has been described by

# 'Everyone knew that bastards were wanton and treacherous by nature, having been born of lust and deceit'

Thoughts of Jon Snow, *A Storm of Swords*[18]

modern historians as tantamount to genocide. Crops were burned, entire villages destroyed, and some estimates claim that as much as 75 per cent of the region's population was either killed or displaced. Powerful he may be, but Ramsay can only aspire to such chaos.

For Jon, the chances of ever attaining real power are negligible, leading to his decision to leave Winterfell and join the Night's Watch. Of course, he is still the child of nobility, so his situation isn't quite as bad as that of a common-born bastard, either in Westeros or in many parts of medieval Europe. As historian Ondřej Schmidt writes: 'from birth they were subjected to all manner of restrictions, discrimination and prejudice', but he goes on to say that 'members of the upper nobility ... were assured a certain privileged status, which allowed them to outstrip illegitimate children from a more humble social background', and also that 'there were ... substantial differences between individual areas in late medieval Europe; in fourteenth- and fifteenth-century Italy we find a whole range of ruling bastard princes'.[19]

A medieval bastard's chances, then, relied on multiple factors: the wealth and status of his father, that father's willingness to recognize (and financially support) their illegitimate child, plus the mores and customs of the region in which they happened to be born. The same is true of Westeros: in Dorne, for example, bastardy is entirely lacking in social stigma; the 'red viper' Oberyn Martell has no less than eight illegitimate daughters, and each of them is powerful in her own way.

For George R.R. Martin, however, it'll always be the downtrodden, luckless ones who hold the closest place in his heart. As he told the Edinburgh Literary Festival in 2014: 'I am attracted to bastards, cripples and broken things ... Outcasts, second-class citizens for whatever reason. There's more drama in characters like that.'[20] And yet, perhaps the most broken character in *A Song of Ice and Fire* isn't a bastard at all, at least not in the literal sense. In fact, he's a prince – of one of the most brutal and unforgiving places in the known world.

Beast in human form: Iwan Rheon as the vicious Ramsay Bolton in *Game of Thrones*

## Chapter Three

# THE IRON ISLANDS

Bayonne, New Jersey, is a port town – not a major hub, perhaps, but a busy harbour, at least at the time George R.R. Martin was growing up there. His father was a dockworker, his family had built the nearby Brady Dock, and he loved to spend his summers splashing in the shallows of the Kill Van Kull, the tidal river that runs past the town, connecting Newark Bay with the New York Harbour. It's hardly surprising, then, that ships and the sea would come to play a central role in his work, from the Mississippi steamboats of his second novel, *Fevre Dream*, to the great merchantmen and warships that ply the unpredictable waters around Westeros, notably the swift longships built and captained by those 'wolves of the sea',[1] the Ironborn.

The historical roots of the people of the Iron Islands are blindingly obvious, even to the casual reader. They travel in open boats, crewed by oarsmen and warriors in furs and armour, armed with swords, clubs and axes. They have names like Erik Ironmaker, Wulfe One-Ear and Andrik the Unsmiling. And they are ruthlessly violent, as their estranged prince, Theon Greyjoy, reflects: 'War was an ironman's proper trade. The Drowned God had made them to reave and rape, to carve out kingdoms and write their names in fire and blood and song.'[2]

They are, of course, Vikings in all but name: Norsemen, like those who sailed from Scandinavia from roughly the eighth to the eleventh centuries to raid and trade throughout Europe, but also as far afield as the Middle East, North Africa and even the shores of North America, where they established the first European colony, known as Vinland. The Vikings were undoubtedly a warlike people – accounts of their savagery are commonplace in the medieval histories, and much of their wealth was built on the capture and trading of slaves. But the Norsemen also had a rich culture, filled with art, songs and stories, and, of course, a diverse pantheon of Gods.

The word 'viking' is actually a retroactive term, applied by the historians of the eighteenth century to describe the Norse tribes of centuries past. The precise roots of the word are unclear, though many modern scholars now believe that it may have been more of a professional description than an inherited identity – like pirates and, indeed, warriors throughout history, these tribesmen would take up 'viking' for a temporary period, then afterwards return to their families, villages and regular trades.

In modern parlance, however, the meaning of Viking is never in doubt, immediately conjuring up images of bearded men in giant ships quaffing mead and wearing little round helmets, with or without horns on. Whether they're depicted as noble savages, comical barbarians or murderous brutes, the iconography is always much the same, and it shares plenty with Martin's vision of the Ironborn.

Like the Vikings, the Ironborn become 'blood-drunk in battle, so berserk that they felt no pain and feared no foe'.[3] Like the Vikings, their roots lie in the north: as Balon Greyjoy tells his son, 'Hard places breed hard men, and hard men rule the world'.[4] Both cultures keep slaves known as *thralls*; and both have a peasant class (to the Vikings, *karls*) and an aristocratic class (*jarls*). Unlike the Vikings, but in keeping with the traditions of Westeros, the Ironborn follow a king, but they also practise a form of rough democracy: the Kingsmoot, traditionally gathered to choose the next monarch and presumably inspired by the great assembly of medieval Iceland known as the *Althing*, one of the oldest parliaments in the world.

Martin has admitted that 'I did take a semester of Scandinavian history back in my sophomore year in college … I read a couple of Icelandic sagas … but after the passage of 30 years I confess I no longer recall the titles or the names of any of the characters'.[5] And, as we learn more

# 'We are as the gods made us … strong and weak, good and bad, cruel and kind, heroic and selfish'

Septon Barth, *Fire and Blood*[6]

about the Ironborn in *A Song of Ice and Fire*, it remains unclear how much of their lifestyle is inspired by real Viking history and culture, and how much by their depiction in popular culture.

In *A Feast for Crows*, for instance, we learn of King Balon Greyjoy that 'at 13, he could run a longship's oars':[7] the act of leaping from oar blade to oar blade along the outside of a ship. This image was made famous by Kirk Douglas in the 1958 Technicolor epic *The Vikings*, released when George R.R. Martin was an impressionable 10-year-old. That film would unleash a wave of Viking adventures into cinemas, from relatively high-grade Hollywood fare like *The Long Ships* (1964) starring Sidney Poitier, to an entire horde of Italian Norsesploitation oddities with titles like *Attack of the Normans* (1962) and *Knives of the Avenger* (1966).

This renewed popularity of all things Norse would also inspire the creation, in 1962, of Marvel's Viking-inspired superhero, Thor, at a time when the young Martin was consuming comic books by the bucketload. At the other end of the bookshelf, Vikings would also become a staple of historical fiction: among the favourite authors listed on George R.R. Martin's 'Reading Recommendations' blog post, several have written books set in the Viking period, notably Cecelia Holland,

with her Corban Loosestrife series (2002–10), and of course 'the incomparable Bernard Cornwell',[8] whose *The Last Kingdom* (2004) and its successors have inspired an enormously popular TV series, which premiered in 2015 and was inevitably likened to HBO's *Game of Thrones*.

In one area, however, the Ironborn differ markedly from the Vikings, whether historical or fictional. The Norsemen – at least before their conversion to Christianity – worshipped a colourful pantheon of jostling deities, from the troublesome trickster Loki to the one-eyed, all-seeing Odin. Whereas the religion of the Ironborn allows for just two gods: the Drowned God, in whose watery, Valhalla-like halls the soul of a slain warrior is said to feast, 'with mermaids to attend his every want':[9] and the Storm God, 'a malignant deity who dwells in the sky and hates men and all their works'.[10] Reflecting the harsh nature of the landscape in which his followers' dwell, the Drowned God is an austere and unforgiving creator, allowing 'no temples, no holy books, no idols carved in his likeness', and demanding that his priests remain homeless and barefoot as they travel the islands spreading his holy word.

Still, at least the Drowned God has a name, which is more than can be said for the other divinities of the North, the Old Gods. Worshipped by the Starks, 'the Old Gods of the First Men and the children of the forest are nameless and numerous',[11] worshipped not in churches but in a godswood, before a giant weirwood tree, carved long before the First Men came to Westeros. It is an animistic religion devoted to 'the innumerable gods of the streams, forests and stones', and practised not just by the men of the North but also the Wildlings beyond the Wall. The religion of the Old Gods might be compared to the ancient druidic religions of pre-Roman Britain and to the pagan religions of the Anglo-Saxon period, which bore many similarities with the Norse religion (they also worshipped Odin, though they knew him as Woden), but also incorporated elements of magic and a belief in elves and dragons.

Norsing about: father and son raiders Ernest Borgnine (left) and Kirk Douglas (right) decide the fate of prize captive Janet Leigh (centre) in 1958's *The Vikings*

'GIVE ME PRIESTS WHO ARE FAT AND CORRUPT AND CYNICAL ... IT'S THE ONES WHO BELIEVE IN GODS WHO MAKE THE TROUBLE'

Tyrion Lannister, *A Dance With Dragons*[12]

Places of worship: Theon Greyjoy (Alfie Allen) prepares to be drowned and reborn in *Game of Thrones* (top), while Jon Snow (Kit Harington) kneels before a weirwood tree (bottom)

These ancient pagan religions would, of course, be largely wiped out by the arrival of Christianity, and indeed a similar process has been at work in Westeros, as the Faith of the Seven, brought to the continent some centuries previously by the invading Andals, works to drive out the faith of the Old Gods. Here, we find evidence of George R.R. Martin's own religious background: with its great stone septs, clouds of incense, flocks of Silent Sisters, pampered, gold-draped High Septons and endless moral statutes, the Faith of the Seven clearly resembles Catholicism, both the medieval religion and its modern-day variation. Both worship a deity who is at once singular and manifold, whether that's the Seven Who Are One or the Holy Trinity; both have amassed huge wealth under the guise of piety; and both have historically encouraged their followers to take up arms in defence of their religion.

And yet, despite its ubiquitous nature across much of Westeros, the Faith of the Seven does not seem to hold anything like the stranglehold over the popular imagination that the Catholic Church did in medieval times. As Professor Larrington writes: 'The Faith of the Seven is curiously sidelined within the power structures of King's Landing. The High Septon has no seat on the Small Council, nor does anyone see fit to consult him or call upon his services except for weddings, coronations and funerals.'[13] Indeed, while a handful of characters – perhaps most notably Sansa Stark and her mother Catelyn – take the tenets of their faith seriously, the majority appear to treat religion rather more pragmatically, exploiting it whenever it becomes convenient – as Cersei does when she reports Margaery Tyrell's alleged malfeasances to the High Septon – and largely ignoring it the rest of the time. It certainly doesn't prevent them from murdering one another in cold blood.

It's only in the wake of the War of the Five Kings that religion in Westeros begins to reassert itself. Named for 'the most common of birds',[14] the movement known as the Sparrows – led by a nameless Septon whose inspiration must surely be the radical, roving preacher John Ball, one of the leaders of the fourteenth-century Peasants' Revolt – is initially a popular uprising, before being legitimized by Cersei Lannister in a rash act of short-term expediency. But, even here, the motives of the man who comes to be known as the High Sparrow remain murky: is he truly Godly, or does he simply seek power, revenge for the crimes committed against his church, and the opportunity to punish those he views as sinners? Either way, whether he'll ultimately suffer the same fate as the aforementioned Ball – who was arrested, decapitated, cut into quarters and distributed across England – remains to be seen.

Of course, the cynicism displayed by many of Westeros's more powerful figures may also have been true of their real-world forebears – there were undoubtedly many in the Middle Ages who paid lip service to their faith while at the same time committing acts of horrific cruelty. And yet, the absolute primacy of religion in the lives of the vast majority of medieval people cannot be doubted: religion was the force that kept kings on their thrones and peasants in their places, driving nobles and ordinary people alike to abandon their settled lives in order to risk life and limb on dangerous pilgrimages to the Holy Land. By contrast, the idea of almost any Westerosi aristocrat abandoning their comfortable castles and setting off to Qarth or Astapor on a mission from God is completely unthinkable.

However, there is one religion in *A Song of Ice and Fire* that not only demands true commitment from its worshippers, but rewards that commitment with genuine miracles: that of the red god R'hllor, the Lord of Light. This name surely pays homage to another great sci-fi novel, the Hugo-winning 1967 religious satire, *Lord of Light,* by Martin's Sante Fe neighbour, Roger Zelazny. Though primarily found in Essos, missionaries from this dualistic religion have begun to make their way across the Narrow Sea, notably Melisandre of Asshai, the Red Priestess, who believes that Stannis Baratheon is the long-prophesied hero, Azor Ahai, reborn.

**ABOVE**
A drawing of Woden surrounded by his descendants, from the twelfth-century manuscript known to historians as 'Cotton Caligula A.'

**OPPOSITE**
John Ball leads the Peasants' Revolt in this illustration from *Chroniques de France et d'Angleterre* by Jean Froissart, c. 1460–80

*Pl. LXVI.*

*A Knight of the 13.ᵗʰ Century? in his Military Habit.*

# 'IT IS DEATH WE CHOOSE, OR LIFE. DARKNESS, OR LIGHT.'

Lady Melisandre, *A Storm of Swords*[15]

# 'WHAT IS DEAD MAY NEVER DIE'

Aeron Greyjoy, *A Clash of Kings*[16]

PRISE DE LAVAUR. — *Composition et dessin de G. Rochegrosse.*

**OPPOSITE**
Hilltop fortress:
the French castle
of Montségur is
said to have been
home to the
Cathar sect

**ABOVE**
The bloody thirteenth-
century sack of the
'heretical' French
town of Lavaur, from
an illustration by
Georges Rochegrosse

With its resurrection rituals and flaming swords, the faith of R'hllor may feel rather more fantastical than the other religions of Westeros, but it, too, has real-world influences. The adherents of the ancient Indo-Iranian religion of Zoroastrianism also worship a being of light and life: *Ahura Mazda*, the Lord of Wisdom. Founded by the prophet Zoroaster (or Zarathustra) in the sixth century BC, the faith survives to this day, particularly in India, and recently celebrated its 3,000th anniversary. Like the followers of R'hllor, Zoroastrian worshippers also utilize fire in their religious ceremonies – Zoroastrian churches are known as Fire Temples, and anyone entering is asked to make an offering of wood to the constantly burning flames.

Another binary faith that may well have inspired Martin was that of the Cathars, a branch of Christianity that apparently emerged sometime in eleventh-century France and was brutally wiped out by the Catholic Church around three centuries later. Though they venerated Jesus and called themselves 'good Christians', most Cathars also believed that there were two gods, one benevolent and the other evil – and it was the latter who had created the world and everyone in it.

This dualistic belief is what turned the Catholics against them, sparking the brutal Albigensian Crusade of the thirteenth century, instigated by Pope Innocent II and intended to wipe out all traces of the Cathars. However, the exact nature of Catharism is still hotly debated. Was it an organized religion at all? Did Cathar priests go about espousing ideas of dualistic worship? Or was this all just rumour and misinformation spread by the Catholic Church as a pretext for committing genocide against a group of wealthy and successful rivals?

Either way, George R.R. Martin's readings into French medieval history (and his love of Maurice Druon) would doubtless have introduced him to this mysterious faith and to the religious wars waged against the Cathars. He must also have been aware of the countless conspiracy myths that have sprung up around the Cathars and their extinction, from the investigations of the Nazi Holy Grail enthusiast, Otto Rahn, to bestselling works of pseudo-history, like the infamous *The Holy Blood and the Holy Grail* (1982), itself the inspiration for Dan Brown's enormously popular pulp thriller *The Da Vinci Code* (2003), in which the legacy of the Cathars and the Knights Templar have dire consequences in the modern day.

But those devoted red priests aside, it's hard to ignore the relative inconsequence of religion in *A Song of Ice and Fire*. And this is perhaps attributable to its author's own personal feelings: in 2011, George R.R. Martin described himself as 'an atheist or agnostic. I find religion and spirituality fascinating. I would like to believe this isn't the end and there's something more, but I can't convince the rational part of me that that makes any sense whatsoever.'[17] He has also made no secret of his cynicism towards organized religion – 'are you really gonna kill all these people because a giant invisible guy in the sky told you to?'[18] – and this may lie at the root of his treatment of the subject. For Martin, it may simply be harder to relate to a character who holds an honest belief in a higher power than to a hard-nosed realist who eschews superstition and sees the world as it truly is.

One character who pays homage to the demands of his faith – accepting a baptism by seawater from his uncle Aeron – but whose thoughts, actions and words ('bugger the Drowned God. If he troubles us, I'll drown him again'[19]) betray his absolute lack of interest in any kind of religious morality is, of course, the Prince of the Iron Islands, Theon Greyjoy. The series' ultimate traitor – a crime for which he will pay dearly – Theon has spent half his life as the hostage or 'ward' of Ned Stark, following a failed rebellion by his father and uncles a decade before.

Again, this idea of ensuring peace through the taking of noble hostages has ample real-world precedent: from Ancient Rome, where the children of conquered peoples, like the Gauls, were regularly transported to Rome as captives to ensure their family's acquiescence; to imperial China, where the exchanging of *zhìzǐ* or 'hostage sons' was common practice between rival states. In fourth-century Ireland, the great monarch, Niall, was said to have taken no less than nine rival kings captive, exerting his own power over their kingdoms and earning him the name Niall Noígíallach, or Niall of the Nine Hostages.

But it was in the medieval period that the practice became most common, not just as a way to assert one's authority but, as Adam J. Kosto writes, as 'a means of guarantee used to secure transactions ranging from treaties to wartime commitments to financial transactions'.[20] After all, what better way to encourage someone to keep their word than to hold a knife to their loved one's throat? And, inevitably, a great number of these hostages were children. When young nobleman William Marshal was taken hostage by the twelfth-century English King Stephen in an effort to force his father to surrender Newbury Castle, the king threatened to fire the boy over the battlements if his demands weren't met. (The exact same threat is employed by Jaime Lannister at the siege of Riverrun, as he tells Edmure Tully: 'You'll want your child, I expect. I'll send him to you when he's born. With a trebuchet.'[21]) Though young William's father told the king to do his worst, claiming that 'he did not care about the child, since he still had the anvils and hammers to produce even finer ones',[22] mercifully Stephen relented, and William went on to serve five kings as Earl of Pembroke.

But hostages could be exchanged for more mundane reasons, too. In the thirteenth century, young Philip of Courtenay was offered up by his parents, Emperor Baldwin II of Constantinople and his wife Marie of Brienne (another name Martin seems to have borrowed) to a group of Venetian merchants as collateral on a loan. It would take 10 years to claim the lad back: his mother 'spent a decade travelling Europe trying to gather the capital to repay this loan',[23] before a generous cousin, King Alfonso of Castile, finally paid the Venetians off.

Like Theon, the majority of these hostages would have been kept in conditions suited to their high status: when King Jean of France was captured by the English in 1356 and held hostage for four years, his recorded expenses included 'horses, dogs, falcons, a chess set, a clock ... and various musical instruments'.[24] Theon may resent his decade-long sentence as Ned Stark's prisoner, but in Westeros, just as in medieval England, life for an aristocratic hostage is infinitely preferable to life as a commoner, whether that's the fisherfolk of the Iron Islands, the peasant farmers of the mainland or the teeming, huddled masses of the greatest city on the continent.

**TOP**
A medieval siege catapult, from the fourteenth-century manuscript known as 'Christ Church MS 92'

**BOTTOM**
A stone effigy of Marie of Brienne, from the Basilica of Saint-Denis in France – note the dragons at her feet

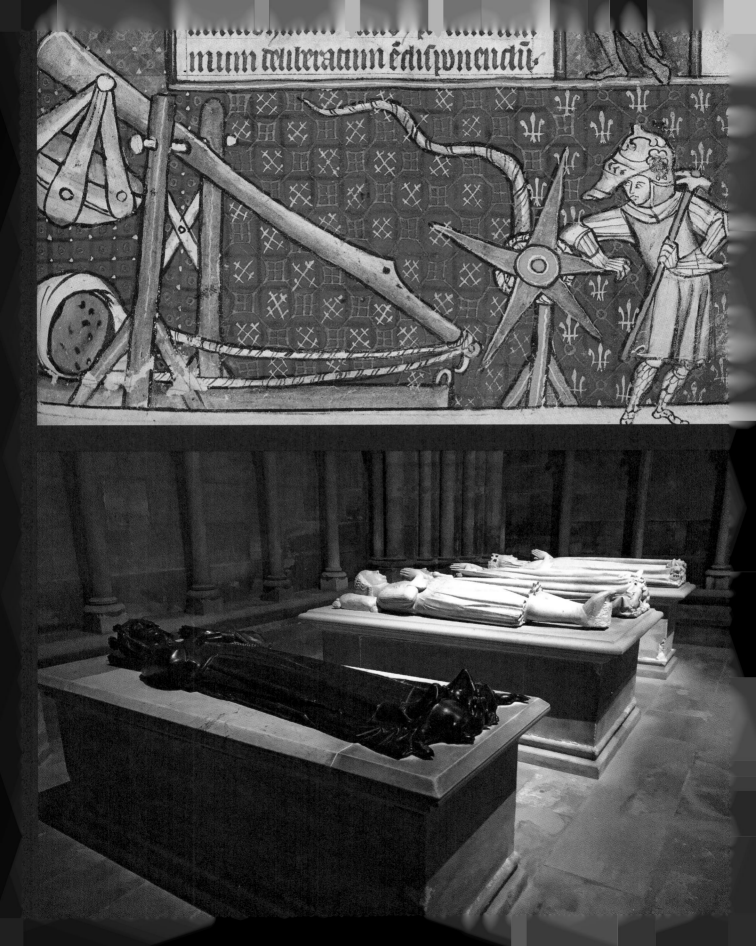

Part Two

# THE
# CROWNLANDS

Chapter Four

# KING'S LANDING

Situated at the mouth of the Blackwater Rush where the river meets the Narrow Sea, the city of King's Landing was built on the site where Aegon the Conqueror first set foot on Westerosi soil to begin his invasion. Ringed with high defensive walls, the city is dominated by three hills, one crowned by the now-derelict Dragonpit, one by the Great Sept of Baelor and one by the Red Keep, a monstrous castle built of impregnable sandstone. Between these three vantage points lie a sprawling multitude of lesser buildings: guildhalls, merchants' warehouses and armouries; wine sinks, kitchens and brothels; and, of course, thousands of dwellings, from wealthy manses to the meanest hovels, many of them lying in the great slum known as Flea Bottom or, for the very poorest, outside the city walls.

King's Landing isn't explicitly modelled on any one city. There are elements of medieval London: both lie on the banks of a river with access to the sea, and there are clear similarities between the Tower of London and the Red Keep, both of which contain both royal residences and prison cells. There's also a physical resemblance between the Sept of Baelor and St Paul's Cathedral, though the domed shape of the Sept is actually closer to the modern version of St Paul's, built after the first

cathedral was destroyed in the Great Fire of London. But in size and population, the Westerosi capital far outstrips the British: 'King's Landing is more populous than medieval London or Paris,' Martin has claimed, 'but not so populous as medieval Constantinople or ancient Rome.'[1] That leaves King's Landing with a population of more than 80,000 but fewer than 2 million: a wide margin of error, perhaps, but at least we know that it is *big*.

Overall, the average medieval-European city-dweller would find themselves right at home in King's Landing. The food would be familiar, with the wealthy dining well on red meat, wildfowl and rich sauces while the medieval poor subsisted largely on cabbage, grains and pottage – a thick soup very similar to the 'bowls o' brown' served in Flea Bottom. The city would even smell like home: as Arya roams the 'narrow crooked unpaved streets' in the wake of her father's arrest, she finds that 'the Bottom had a stench to it, a stink of pigsties and stables and tanner's sheds, mixed in with the sour smell of wine sinks and cheap whorehouses'.[2]

Brothels were certainly common in the medieval period, just as they are in King's Landing. Though sex work was officially outlawed within the walls of London in 1310 – with any 'common woman' caught

practising the trade liable for up to 40 days in prison – in fact, prostitution was just driven further underground, and by the end of the century had sprung up again, principally in the appropriately named Cokkes Lane in Smithfield. But, as in King's Landing, it wasn't the sex workers themselves who profited most, but those men who oversaw the trade, among them the fifteenth-century Bishop of Winchester, who laid down a list of fines on prostitution. 'So profitable did this venture prove,' writes historian Kate Lister, 'that the sex workers of Southwark came to be known as "Winchester Geese".'[3]

Indeed, the medieval church's position on sex work wasn't as cut and dried as one might expect. Across Europe, prostitution was largely tolerated, with many subscribing to Saint Augustine's maxim: 'suppress prostitution, and capricious lusts will overthrow society.'[4] But although medieval brothels often offered bathing services – as a result of which they came to be known as 'stewhouses' or 'stews' – the existence of brothels as plush and glamorous as those owned by Petyr Baelish is dubious. Most historians agree that medieval sex work was an ugly trade, 'a marginal world that was for most dominated by poverty, violence, deprivation and crime ... within a society whose laws were created and enforced by

The mighty Red Keep
of King's Landing,
as imagined in Game
of Thrones

# 'BROTHELS ARE A MUCH SOUNDER INVESTMENT THAN SHIPS, I'VE FOUND. WHORES SELDOM SINK.'

Petyr Baelish, *A Game of Thrones*[5]

# 'I AM SURROUNDED BY FLATTERERS AND FOOLS. IT CAN DRIVE A MAN TO MADNESS.'

Robert Baratheon, *A Game of Thrones*[6]

men who in general considered women to be a subordinate species.'[7] Punishments for those women who broke the rules could be brutal and humiliating, from having their nostrils slit to being strapped into the *thewe*, or ducking chair.

However, *A Song of Ice and Fire* isn't really about sex workers, or slum dwellers, or anyone else below the poverty line. Though these characters may play their part, the focus of the story remains squarely on the nobility: even when Martin does give voice to a low-born character, like Lord Varys, or Flea Bottom's very own jumped-up smuggler, Davos Seaworth, we only hear from them *after* they've been elevated to a position of power. The vast majority of King's Landing's population remains entirely faceless – 'the unshaven and the unwashed … a sea of ragged men and hungry women'[8] – ridden roughshod over by their lords, at least until they rise up, form an angry mob and begin hurling abuse and faeces. A low-born docker's son himself, Martin's empathy for these 'smallfolk' is never in doubt – as the humble Septon Meribald says, 'it is being common-born that is dangerous, when the great lords play their game of thrones'[9] – but, nonetheless, it is behind thick stone walls that the real action of the story takes place.

As battles rage across Westeros and beyond, within the Red Keep the atmosphere is no less fraught, as the members of the Royal Court connive either to seize the Iron Throne for themselves or to secure it for their chosen successor. And, of course, tales of courtly intrigue form the bedrock not just of most historical fiction but of large swathes of real history, as significant as outright war in shaping the destiny of kingdoms.

Perhaps the most subtle and devious player of the game of thrones is Varys, the lowborn eunuch and Master of Whisperers who serves under both Robert Baratheon and his 'son' King Joffrey. His closest historical parallel might be the sixteenth-century secretary of state, Francis Walsingham, who, like Varys, rose from humble origins to become trusted spymaster to Queen Elizabeth I. A scheming manipulator whose 'highly effective intelligence network … successfully thwarted England's foreign enemies and exposed domestic plotters who sought to unseat Elizabeth',[10] Walsingham was a cautious and strategic thinker whose philosophy appears to have been summed up in the words he wrote in a letter to his contemporary, Sir William Cecil: 'there is lesse daynger in fearinge to much then too lyttle.'[11]

But, for the most part, it was not the courtiers but the royals themselves whose marriages, affairs, betrayals and revenges would shape the fortunes of the kingdoms they reigned over. For example, while the

The queen's spymaster: this sixteenth-century portrait of Sir Francis Walsingham is attributed to John de Critz

·EDWARD·II·

·HENRY·IV·

·HENRY·V·

·HENRY·VI·

·EDWARD·IV·

·HENRY·VIII·

# 'Some men are like swords, made for fighting. Hang them up and they go to rust.'

Donal Noye, *A Clash of Kings*[12]

arranged marriage of Edward II of England to Isabella the She-Wolf of France may, like the wedding of Cersei Lannister to Robert Baratheon, have seemed profitable for both parties at the time, Edward's lack of interest in Isabella's womanly charms and her propensity for taking other lovers ultimately drove the couple apart. This led to Isabella deposing (and, some historians argue, to murdering) Edward II so that their young son, Edward III, could take the throne, with herself acting – as Cersei does during the reign of her son Tommen – as the queen regent.

But poor Edward II isn't the only possible inspiration for King Robert Baratheon. In fact, scholars have pointed to no less than five other English monarchs – all but one, rather confusingly, named Henry – whose exploits and/or personalities mirror Robert's to a lesser or greater degree. Like Robert, Henry IV, the great-grandson of Edward, overthrew the reigning monarch, Richard II, and took his throne, thereby setting in motion a bloody conflict, the Wars of the Roses. His son, Henry V, was a legendary warrior who smashed the French at Agincourt but who, like Robert, displayed a notable indifference towards domestic affairs. His son, Henry VI, most resembles the older, fading Robert that we meet in *A Game of Thrones* – an inept, ineffectual monarch with a fiercely ambitious wife, Margaret of Anjou. However, it was widely claimed that Henry VI suffered from a severe mental illness, which is not the case with Robert Baratheon.

Henry's Yorkist successor, Edward IV, takes us back to the younger Robert: a strapping lad almost 1.9 m (6 ft 4 in) in height who was, as Sir Thomas More observes: 'very princely to behold ... in peace just and merciful, in war sharp and fierce, in the field bold and hardy, and nevertheless no further than wisdom would, adventurous.' More does note, however, that while 'he was of visage lovely; of body mighty, strong and clean made; howbeit in his latter days, with over liberal diet, [he became] somewhat corpulent and burly'.[13] The same description might also apply to the last of Robert's regal ancestors: Henry VIII, another dashing young monarch – the Venetian ambassador described him as 'the handsomest potentate I ever set eyes on; above the usual height, with an extremely fine calf to his leg'[14] – whose profligate spending and bodily appetites were legendary, along with his increasingly expanding waistline.

But the treacherous schemes carried out by the members of the Westerosi court might also display the influence of a rather less aristocratic band of courtiers. Before he began writing *A Song of Ice and Fire*, George R.R. Martin had been employed for some years as a TV writer, and indeed his relationship with the small screen goes right back to childhood: '*Howdy Doody* on Saturday mornings, and cartoons every day of the week ... *Robin Hood* and *Ivanhoe* and *Sir Lancelot*.'[15] But when two young TV producers called David Benioff and D.B. Weiss came – with Martin's blessing – to pitch a small-screen adaptation of *A Song of Ice and Fire* to the American networks, it was a more recent series that they used as a convenient

King Robert's ancestors: six English monarchs from the stained glass windows at Bridgnorth Town Hall in Shropshire

# 'In the songs all knights are gallant, all maids are beautiful, and the sun is always shining'

Brienne of Tarth, *A Clash of Kings*[16]

shorthand: as Martin recalled later, 'Their pitch was *The Sopranos* in Middle Earth'.[17]

While it's true that creator David Chase's long-running mafia drama didn't actually premiere until 1999, by which time George R.R. Martin was two books into his fantasy epic, it's easy to find parallels between the feuding 'court' of small-time criminals presided over by Tony Soprano and its more regal Westerosi equivalent, particularly when it comes to their loose morals. And there's no doubt that George R.R. Martin is a *Sopranos* fan: 'Characters don't have to be likeable, they just have to be interesting,' he told an audience at the Toronto International Film Festival in 2012. 'Tony Soprano is an immensely likeable guy and he's also a thoroughly scumbag sociopath [sic]. [But] it was hard not to feel for Tony. Some of the people he was dealing with were a lot worse than he was.'[18] In that description, we might hear an echo of characters like Robert, Jaime Lannister or even his brother Tyrion: figures who, though they may commit terrible acts, are surrounded by genuinely monstrous, rapacious villains.

Television also taught George R.R. Martin valuable lessons about storytelling, as he revealed to *Time* magazine in 2011. 'Network TV requires people to come back after the commercial ... you always want

to have an act break that's a moment of revelation, a twist, a moment of tension, a cliffhanger. I want to keep people turning the pages ... so I tried to end every chapter with an act break.' That sense of constant forwards motion, of a story with so much momentum that one is left with no choice but to keep reading, is vital to the power and popularity of *A Song of Ice and Fire*.

Besides the royal court, there is another place where the great and the good of Westeros vie for dominance, and where fortunes large and small can be won and lost: the tournament ground. And while for much of *A Song of Ice and Fire* the knights of the realm are too busy fighting actual wars to indulge in proxy ones,[19] we are constantly being reminded of their historical importance. It was at the great tournament at Harrenhal that Prince Rhaegar Targaryen gave his favour to Lyanna Stark, ultimately sparking Robert's rebellion. And much of the first episode of the Martin-produced prequel series *House of the Dragon* (2022) focuses on a magnificent tourney at King's Landing to celebrate the impending birth of the royal heir.

But, in the medieval period, such tournaments were not just about spectacle and violence, the equivalent of a boxing match or even of Roman-style gladiatorial combat. They were also a key part of the

**TOP**
A public spectacle: the tournament in King's Landing from the opening episode of *House of the Dragon*

**BOTTOM**
'Scumbag sociopath': Tony Soprano (James Gandolfini, centre) with his crew in *The Sopranos*

Il celle saison et entretant que les treuces se tenoi ent en france et en angleterre par mer et par terre que le puis Samuertine en recep uoit les plantes en venoient a pure eut conseil le voy de fran ce deuoyer deuers le voy dauglё terre et luu escripre et sigmifier

chivalric tradition, that set of rules and guidelines for the behaviour of knights, lords and warriors, laid down in the Middle Ages, and gleefully unpicked by George R.R. Martin throughout *A Song of Ice and Fire*. In large part the work of the clergy, the rules of chivalry sought to introduce the armed nobility to 'Christian behaviours like defending the weak, fighting against the wicked, deference to women, telling the truth and offering a fair fight to the opponent'.[20]

After all, in the medieval period the term 'knight' as we understand it – to mean a mounted warrior in service to a king or other authority – was relatively recent: the idea of 'knighting' someone appears as late as the fourteenth century. And these newly minted knights were often descended from fairly brutal ancestors: for example, the Norman knights who invaded England in 1066 were just a few generations removed from a band of Nordic raiders – essentially Vikings – who had conquered and settled parts of Northern France. Chivalry was intended to offer a set of rules to live by, to keep them from indulging in petty in-fighting and bloody wars for conquest. These values were then seeded into great romantic tales like *The Song of Roland* (*c.* 1040–1115) and the legends of King Arthur, offering knights and kings a set of heroes to live up to.

In Westeros, too, stories from the mythic 'Age of Heroes' are widely read, particularly by impressionable young girls like Sansa Stark – who thrills to the tale of Florian the Fool and his lady Jonquil – and young Rhaenyra Targaryen in *House of the Dragon*, who imagines herself as Princess Nymeria, conqueror of Dorne. The more cynical characters may scorn such stories – the Hound bluntly describes Florian and Jonquil as 'a fool and his c***'[21] – but they are nonetheless familiar with the same legends, which form a vital part of the cultural tapestry of the Seven Kingdoms.

The chivalric tradition was particularly popular in medieval France – the word chivalry derives from the French *chevalier*, meaning knight, and the majority of romance literature was French in origin. But the tales of Arthur were also widely retold in England, leading to a renewed popularity of the idea of noble castes, like the Order of the Garter, founded by Edward III in 1348 and explicitly inspired by Arthur and his Knights of the Round Table. In Westeros, the equivalent order is the Sworn Brotherhood of the Kingsguard, forged by Queen Visenya in the year 4AC to protect and defend her brother, Aegon the Conqueror: 'seven champions for the Lord of the Seven Kingdoms ... they would forfeit all things save their duty to the King.'[22]

**LEFT**
Edward III, founder of
the Order of the Garter,
from the 'William Bruges
Garter Book', *c.* 1450

**RIGHT**
The myth of chivalry:
Edmund Leighton's
1900 painting *God Speed*
depicts a noble lady
bidding farewell to
her brave knight

**OPPOSITE**
Protector of the realm:
Paddy Considine as King
Viserys II Targaryen in
*House of the Dragon*

# 'IT IS CHIVALRY WHICH MAKES A TRUE KNIGHT, NOT A SWORD'

Sir Barristan Selmy, *A Dance With Dragons*[23]

**OPPOSITE**
Harsh reality: Ser
Meryn Trant (Ian
Beattie) abuses Sansa
Stark (Sophie Turner)
on the orders of his king
in *Game of Thrones*

**ABOVE**
Toy soldier: A miniature
medieval pikeman

But neither organization has an unblemished record. 'In order for the Garter to be honourable,' writes Professor Jonathan Good, 'it needed to threaten and occasionally punish members ... if they took up arms against a fellow knight, or if they were found to be heretical, traitorous, or cowardly in battle.'[24] Such punishments could range from degradation – the removal of knightly honour – to execution, and, indeed, over the centuries no less than 36 members of the Order of the Garter have had their heads removed for various reasons. Other members of the Order whose actions would seem to run counter to their stated tradition of chivalry and honour include Kaiser Wilhelm II, who ruled Germany during the First World War; Emperor Hirohito of Japan; and Prince Andrew, Duke of York.

Similarly, the Kingsguard are nowhere near as noble in reality as they may have been in intention. By the time of King Joffrey, they have become a somewhat unsavoury bunch whose ranks include the child-murdering Sandor Clegane, the cowardly Ser Boros Blount, 'an ugly man with a foul temper, all scowls and jowls',[25] and Ser Meryn Trant, who beats the teenage Sansa bloody on the orders of his king. And it's largely through Sansa's eyes that we see the myth of chivalry exposed, as time and again those she perceives as noble – from Joffrey himself to her own Florian, Ser Dontos – turn out to be brutish, treacherous or simply ineffectual.

But for George R.R. Martin, knights don't exist simply as figures from history or heroes in storybooks. 'Like all red-blooded American boys, I had a Marx castle and some plastic toy knights as a kid,' he writes on his website. 'But in 1996, deep in the throes of writing my fantasy series, my old passions reawakened, and I started buying toy knights once again.'[26] In the years since, his collection of miniature horsemen has grown inexorably, as has his expertise in the field. Martin's website doesn't just feature extensive photography of his favourite figurines, but informative and enthusiastic writing on the history of the form and its key exponents, including 'the master', Richard Courtenay, several of whose 'exquisitely sculpted 54 mm [2 in] knights painted in authentic heraldry'[27] Martin considers himself lucky to own.

Over the years he has been given several pieces based on characters from his stories – including a 'magnificent' figure of the young Robert Baratheon, 'specially commissioned by my fair lady Parris as a Christmas gift'[28] – and in 2005 and 2007 signed agreements with miniature producers to create figures based on a variety of characters from the series, including Jaime and Cersei, the Hound, Melisandre and Jon Snow. His heart, however, remains firmly in the Middle Ages: 'The focus of my collection is strictly medieval,' he writes. 'I collect plastic, lead, pewter, and composition figures; painted and unpainted; old and new; cheap plastic recasts of old Marx and Ideal knights from the '50s to the current masterpieces coming out of Russia, and everything in between.'[29] The roots of this collection go all the way back to the days of Turtle Castle (see page 7), and it's easy to imagine how collecting and painting these figurines – along with their horses, weapons, armour and even entire castles and villages – has enabled the author to more deeply enter the world of *A Song of Ice and Fire*.

Chapter Five

# DRAGONSTONE

Situated off the coast of Westeros in the mouth of Blackwater Bay, the storm-tossed island of Dragonstone – and the monolithic castle that occupies its peak – has been the ancestral seat of the Targaryen family since before the Doom of Old Valyria. It was from Dragonstone that Aegon Targaryen, along with his sisters Visenya and Rhaenys, planned their conquest of Westeros, forging a dynasty that would rule the continent for the next three centuries. And, as seen in *House of the Dragon*, it is to this island sanctuary that Targaryen nobles tend to return whenever danger threatens.

As already discussed, the primary historical inspiration for the Targaryen family were the Capetians (see page 27), the descendants of Hugh Capet – himself a descendant of the Frankish Emperor Charlemagne – who ruled in France from 987 until 1328, making them one of the most enduring royal families in European history. Individual Targaryens, however, have their own historical parallels. Aegon I obviously shares a great deal of his DNA with William the Conqueror, while his descendant, Viserys I – the ailing king in the first season of *House of the Dragon* – would seem to owe much to the popular image of Edward the Confessor, a well-meaning but somewhat ineffectual monarch who left no obvious heir, leading to in-fighting among his potential successors.

However, Martin himself draws a different historical parallel for the events depicted in the spin-off series, which cover the troubled period of Targaryen in-fighting known as the Dance of the Dragons. 'Game of Thrones is, as many people have observed, very loosely based on the War [sic] of the Roses,' he told a Comic-Con audience in 2022. '[*House of the Dragon*] is based on an earlier period in history called the Anarchy.'¹ This statement sent fans scurrying to their history books, eager

to learn exactly what this Anarchy was, and how detectable its influence might be on *House of the Dragon*.

Waged from 1138 until 1153, the Anarchy was a war for the English succession that broke out following the death of King Henry I, who left no obvious heir after the accidental drowning at sea of his only son, William. Like Viserys in *House of the Dragon*, who intends for his daughter Rhaenyra to succeed him, Henry had hoped that his daughter, Empress Matilda, the wife of the future Holy Roman Emperor, Henry V, would be permitted to rule, but, despite having sworn oaths of fealty, the English nobility weren't about to allow a woman onto the throne. Like Viserys, Henry also took a younger bride, presumably hoping for more sons, but it was not to be. Enter Henry's nephew, Stephen of Blois – the same man who threatened to fire a small boy from a trebuchet in Chapter 3 (see page 64) – who seized the throne for himself, forcing supporters of Matilda to declare war against him.

Stephen, then, would presumably be the inspiration behind Aegon II Targaryen: both men took the throne from their aunt, and both have a close relationship with a younger brother – in Stephen's case this was Henry, later to become Bishop of Winchester. The differences are equally

**LEFT**
The heir apparent: Milly Alcock as the young Rhaenyra Targaryen with her mount Syrax in *House of the Dragon*

**RIGHT**
This 1837 portrait by Charles de Steuben depicts Hugh Capet, the founder of one of Europe's great dynasties

# 'MEN WOULD SOONER PUT THE REALM TO THE TORCH THAN SEE A WOMAN ASCEND THE IRON THRONE'

Princess Rhaenys Velaryon, *House of the Dragon*[2]

# 'A QUEEN I AM, BUT MY THRONE IS MADE OF BURNED BONES'

Daenerys Targaryen, *A Dance With Dragons*[3]

notable, however. Aegon is Viserys' natural-born son, not his nephew, and he's hardly a battle leader: sullen, bitter and petulant, Aegon acts largely as a puppet for his mother, Alicent Hightower, and her ambitious father, Ser Otto.

The Anarchy would rage for years, claiming countless lives, before culminating in what was essentially a truce: following the sudden and still unexplained death of his heir, Eustace, Stephen would remain on the throne until his own death – at which point, Matilda's first-born son, Henry, would succeed him. This outcome was a relatively happy one: Henry II would rule for 35 years, and the dynasty he founded – the House of Plantagenet – would go on to transform England.

Of course, there's one Targaryen with whom readers of *A Song of Ice and Fire* – and viewers of *Game of Thrones* – are more familiar than any other: Daenerys Stormborn, Princess of Dragonstone, Queen of the Andals and the Rhoynar and the First Men, Khaleesi of the Great Grass Sea, Breaker of Shackles and Mother of Dragons. Scholars and armchair historians alike have attempted to compare Daenerys to numerous historical figures, from powerful women like Cleopatra – another scion of an incestuous dynasty who fell in love with a conquering warrior – and Olga

of Kiev – who besieged and burned the city of Iskorosten – to male leaders, such as Henry VII, who – like Daenerys – was raised in exile but who was nonetheless able to raise an army and retake the English throne. But while any, or indeed all, of these claims may hold value, what's interesting about Daenerys is not her influences, but her actions. For, as she makes her way along the desert shores of Slaver's Bay, sacking the ancient city of Astapor, threatening the slavers of Yunkai and finally settling in Meereen, Daenerys's long march brings to mind one of the most notoriously bloody and violent periods in all medieval history: the Crusades.

Like Daenerys's conquest of the slave cities, the Crusades were a world-shattering event that no one saw coming. In 1095, with his authority under threat from numerous quarters, including the 'anti-pope' who styled himself Clement III, the legitimately elected Pope Urban II gave a speech at Clermont in France, calling upon the nobles of Europe to aid him in mounting a great Crusade to 'liberate' the Holy Land, and particularly the city of Jerusalem, from the Muslim settlers who had captured the city some four-and-a-half centuries previously. This speech was more successful than he could possibly have expected: a year later, as many as

**TOP**
Crusader's army: Daenerys Targaryen (Emilia Clarke) leads a battalion of Unsullied warriors in *Game of Thrones*

**BOTTOM LEFT**
Anarchy in the UK: a 1380 illustration of Queen Matilda, whose efforts to claim her rightful throne led to civil war

**BOTTOM RIGHT**
Words can kill: Pope Urban II speaks at the Council of Clermont, from a 1490 manuscript illuminated by Sébastien Mamerot

# 'You can have the power to destroy, but it doesn't give you the power to reform, or improve, or build'

George R.R. Martin[4]

100,000 people, from moneyed nobility down to the poorest peasant, had started east, many of them on foot, proceeding across Southern Europe towards Constantinople, through Anatolia and on into the areas we now know as Syria, Lebanon, Israel and Palestine.

The full, bloody history of the Crusades – which lasted some 200 years, and cost hundreds of thousands of lives – is far too complex to go into here, but it is possible to draw several parallels between that real-world catastrophe and the conquests of Daenerys Targaryen. By the time she reaches Meereen, the Mother of Dragons has acquired a retinue of some 80,000 freed slaves, referred to by Ser Jorah as 'mouths with feet',[5] who 'ate the land bare as they passed, like locusts with sandals'.[6] Similarly, during the Crusades, those common-born folk who set off from Europe on foot began to starve once they reached the desert lands of the Middle East, becoming more of a hindrance than a help to their wealthier, better-supplied fellow Crusaders.

To enter Meereen, Daenerys sends Ser Jorah and a team of infiltrators to free a party of slaves and open the gates from inside, allowing her army to enter. Similarly, at the Siege of Antioch, the Italian prince, Bohemond, persuaded one of the commanders of the city's defences,

an Armenian named Firouz, to throw down a rope ladder, allowing Bohemond's forces to sneak inside and open the gates. And when Meereen falls, the result is pure horror: entering the city, Daenerys rides 'past burned buildings and broken windows, through brick streets where the gutters were choked with the stiff and swollen dead'.[7] This is a clear echo of the moment when, after five years, the exhausted survivors of the First Crusade finally took Jerusalem, with appalling results: 'the crusaders began a systematic purge of the city, going into homes and killing anyone they found. Only some captives were spared, so they could carry out the work of removing the dead bodies to outside the walls, and after this they too were executed.'[8]

Like Daenerys, the Crusaders occupied the city, ultimately founding the Kingdom of Jerusalem, one of the four Crusader States or *Outremer* (from the French, meaning 'across the sea') established across the region. But, again like Daenerys, they found it harder to hold on to these regions than it had been to conquer them: just as Astapor and Yunkai are ultimately retaken by the slavers Daenerys defeated, so the Crusader States would one by one fall to a resurgent Muslim force under the Kurdish sultan Salah al-Din Yusuf ibn Ayyub, known as Saladin. Of course, the Crusaders weren't the first or the last foreign army to discover that conquest is easier than occupation: it's also worth noting that *A Storm of Swords* was written in the wake of the Gulf War in 1990–91 and published not long before the 2003 US invasion of Iraq, wars that would begin with avowedly noble intentions and end in guerrilla fighting and widespread insurgency.

But Daenerys has a unique weapon in her arsenal, one that – in the books, at least – she hasn't yet deployed against her enemies. And the metaphorical relevance of dragons in *A Song of Ice and Fire* is clear: like the Ring of Power in Tolkien's *The Lord of the Rings*, they represent the ultimate military capability of their age, whether that's mounted cavalry, catapults, rifles, machine guns or nuclear missiles, the possession and

**OPPOSITE**
Crusader knights in combat with Turkish troops in the illuminated fifteenth-century artwork *Battle of Dorylaeum* by Jean Colombe

**OVERLEAF**
An unholy massacre: the 1847 artwork *Taking of Jerusalem by the Crusaders, 15th July 1099* by Émile Signol

# 'For the first time in hundreds of years, the night came alive with the music of dragons'

George R.R. Martin, *A Game of Thrones*[9]

deployment of which can be as corrupting to the user as to their target. So, while earlier Targaryen conquerors were willing to use dragons as an attacking force – leading to several wholesale massacres, including the Field of Fire, at which thousands of knights and soldiers were burned alive – Daenerys is more cautious, fearing mass casualties and the loss of innocent lives. Instead, she locks her dragons away, preferring – like the superpowers of the Cold War – to keep them as a threat, a sword held over the heads of her enemies.

Martin's dragons are drawn from a multitude of sources: like the dragons and 'wyrms' of Norse and Germanic mythology, they are essentially winged lizards of enormous size, able to breathe fire and raze villages to the ground. Like Smaug in Tolkien's *The Hobbit*, they're also smarter than the average lizard, able to read human emotions and form close bonds with their riders. Unlike Smaug, however, they're unable to speak, uninterested in gold and,

at least in Daenerys's time, somewhat smaller. 'Drogon is a very young dragon,' Martin said in 2014. 'Smaug is gigantic... and would probably have an intellectual advantage. But [Aegon's dragon] Balerion could give Smaug some trouble.'[10]

Perhaps the closest comparison to Martin's dragons derives from rather more niche origins, namely the 1981 Hollywood fantasy *Dragonslayer*, co-written and directed by regular Spielberg collaborator, Matthew Robbins, and set in a pseudo-medieval kingdom under siege by a ferocious dragon. Despite cutting-edge effects and a stunningly realized fire-breathing star, the film was something of a flop. However, it would go on to gather a small but vocal fanbase, among them Oscar-winning director, Guillermo del Toro, who raved about the film's 'perfect creature designs',[11] and Martin himself, who in 2011 named it among his 10 favourite fantasy movies of all time.[12] 'Vermithrax Pejorative is the best dragon ever put on film,' he enthused, 'and has the coolest dragon name as well.'[13]

**ABOVE**
Dragon stone: this runic memorial to King Harald Bluetooth in Jelling churchyard, Denmark, erected *c.* 965, depicts a coiled serpent

**OPPOSITE**
'The best dragon ever put on film': the mighty Vermithrax Pejorative in *Dragonslayer* (1981)

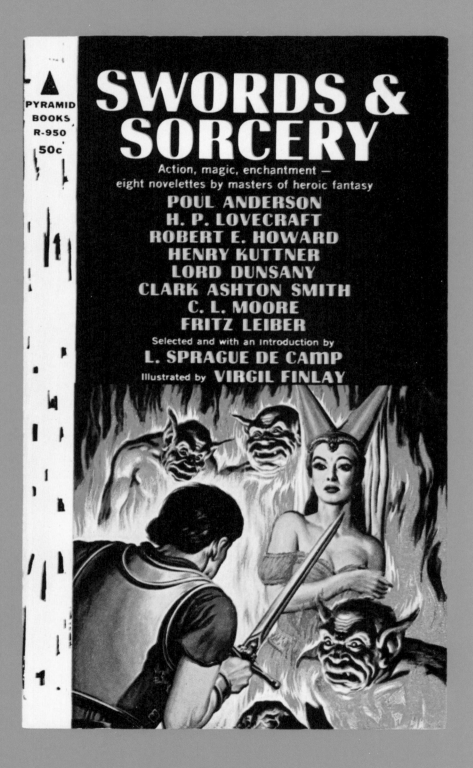

SWORDS &
SORCERY

Action, magic, enchantment —
eight novelettes by masters of heroic fantasy

POUL ANDERSON
H. P. LOVECRAFT
ROBERT E. HOWARD
HENRY KUTTNER
LORD DUNSANY
CLARK ASHTON SMITH
C. L. MOORE
FRITZ LEIBER

Selected and with an introduction by
L. SPRAGUE DE CAMP

Illustrated by VIRGIL FINLAY

PYRAMID
BOOKS
R-950
50c

It is in the depiction of the dragons that *A Song of Ice and Fire* feels most like a work of traditional fantasy fiction – but things could have been very different. When he first came to write *A Game of Thrones*, George R.R. Martin questioned whether he was even writing that sort of book:

> I did consider at a very early stage ... whether to include overt fantasy elements,' [he would tell *Rolling Stone*.] The main question was ... do I include dragons? I was discussing this with a friend ... and she said, 'George, it's a fantasy – you've got to put in the dragons.' She convinced me, and it was the right decision.[14]

George R.R. Martin's history with the fantasy genre goes all the way back to his teenage years, and his purchase of 'a slim Pyramid anthology entitled *Swords & Sorcery* ... inside were stories by Poul Anderson, Henry Kuttner, Clark Ashton Smith, Lord Dunsany and H.P. Lovecraft... Fritz Leiber... and Robert E. Howard.'[15] It was Howard, whose tale 'Shadows in the Moonlight' would most vividly spark the imagination of the young Martin, leading to a lifelong love affair with the creator of Kull the Conqueror and Conan the Barbarian that would inspire much

of his later work (there's a lot of Conan in Khal Drogo, as presumably noted by the producers of the forgettable 2011 *Conan the Barbarian* remake, which cast HBO's very own Drogo, Jason Momoa, in the title role).

But, like just about every other modern writer or indeed reader of the genre, Martin's passion for fantasy would truly come alive when, in 1965, he first discovered J.R.R. Tolkien. Purchasing a bootleg copy of *The Fellowship of the Ring* (1954) from a local newsstand, Martin was at first nonplussed: 'I began to wonder if I had not made a mistake ... What the hell was all this stuff about pipe-weed?' It wasn't long, however, before the book's power began to take effect: 'By the time we got to Weathertop, Tolkien had me.'[16]

But while *The Lord of the Rings* (1954–55) may remain one of his favourite novels, Martin is not a simple Tolkien fanboy. 'As a writer, I was seriously daunted by Tolkien,' he would admit in his story collection, *Dreamsongs* (2003). 'I will never be able to do what he's done, I would think, I will never be able to come close.'[17] And so, when he did finally come to write his own fantasy sequence, Martin decided not to ape Tolkien, but to challenge him. 'As much as I admire him, I do quibble with [Tolkien],' he would say later. '*Lord of the Rings* had a very medieval philosophy,

TWO SOUGHT ADVENTURE
BY FRITZ LEIBER

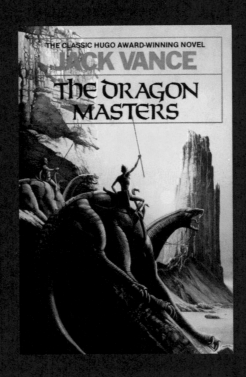
THE CLASSIC HUGO AWARD-WINNING NOVEL
JACK VANCE
THE DRAGON MASTERS

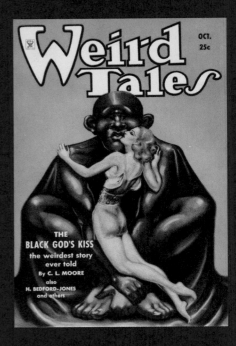
Weird Tales
OCT. 25c
THE BLACK GOD'S KISS
the weirdest story ever told
By C. L. MOORE
also H. BEDFORD-JONES and others

Ursula Le Guin
A WIZARD OF EARTHSEA

Ursula Le Guin
THE TOMBS OF ATUAN

Ursula Le Guin
THE FARTHEST SHORE

that if the king was a good man, the land would prosper. We look at real history and it's not that simple ... In real life, real-life kings had real-life problems to deal with. Just being a good guy was not the answer. You had to make hard, hard decisions.'[18]

It didn't help that, in the wake of *The Lord of the Rings*, a host of far less-talented imitators had cheapened the brand. 'Tolkien had an enormous influence on me, but [then] there was a dark period in the history of epic fantasy where there were a lot of Tolkien imitations coming out that were terrible. I didn't necessarily want to be associated with those books.'[19]

Indeed, many of the fantasy authors listed on Martin's aforementioned 'Reading Recommendations'[20] post (see page 40) were, like Robert E. Howard, writing before Tolkien, or at least before *The Lord of the Rings* hit its peak of popularity in the 1960s. Fritz Leiber, for instance, published his first stories as early as 1943: frequently featuring a pair of loveable rogues named Fafhrd and the Gray Mouser, they were favourites of Martin's from a young age. Likewise, the stories that would make up C.L. Moore's *Jirel of Joiry* collection, about a warrior woman questing across a fantastical version of medieval France, were written between 1935 and 1939.

Even in the dark times, however, chinks of light shone through. When asked in 1999 who his favourite writer was, Martin unhesitatingly replied 'Jack Vance', before going on to praise not just Vance's early work as a sci-fi and fantasy writer – culminating in the cycle of stories known as *The Dying Earth* (1950–84), which fused both genres – but his contemporary writing, too: 'He keeps hitting these home runs as far as I'm concerned, and I can't stop reading him.'[21] Another influence was Tad Williams, and in particular the fantasy trilogy that began with 1988's *The Dragonbone Chair*. 'One of the things that really set me to write [*A Song of Ice and Fire*] was Tad Williams's series ... *Memory, Sorrow, and Thorn*. I remember reading that and saying, you know, Tad has really proved here that this sort of thing doesn't have to

be the province of badly written, derivative books.'[22]

Martin also praises Ursula K. Le Guin, whose debut *Rocannon's World* (1966) fuses sci-fi with sorcery and whose magnificent *Earthsea* series (1968–2001) he singles out for particular acclaim. It's a more obscure Le Guin work, however, whose influence might be most clearly detectable in *A Game of Thrones*. *Planet of Exile* (1966) is set on the third planet of the Gamma Draconis system, a world occupied both by nomadic tribes of indigenous peoples and by marooned settlers from Earth. But the world is facing an ecological catastrophe: with such a wide planetary orbit that a full seasonal cycle can take 60 years to complete, the inhabitants find themselves facing a winter lasting decades. Along with sci-fi writer Brian Aldiss's *Helliconia* quartet (1982–1985), set on the titular world where seasons can endure for centuries, Le Guin's book may well have inspired the long seasons that afflict the world of *A Song of Ice and Fire*.

## Chapter Six
# THE TWINS

Of the innumerable keeps and castles ranged across the Seven Kingdoms, several have names that live in infamy. There's Maegor's Holdfast at the heart of the Red Keep, built by the most bloodthirsty of all the Targaryen kings, Maegor the Cruel, who executed every craftsman so that no one might know its secrets but him. There's the sprawling monstrosity of Harrenhal, built by Harren the Black as a symbol of his power, only to be burned to slag by Aegon the Conqueror and his dragon, Balerion the Black Dread, on the very day the lord took residence. And, of course, there's The Twins, the home of House Frey, whose betrayal and murder of their sworn lord, Robb Stark, will forever be known as the Red Wedding.[1]

For readers of *A Song of Ice and Fire* – and indeed for viewers of the HBO adaptation, who flooded social media with horrified reaction videos the day after the offending episode aired – the Red Wedding is the most shocking event in the entire series: the brutal slaughter of two key characters, Robb Stark and his mother Catelyn,[2] along with their supporters, bannermen and loved ones. Even more than the execution of Ned Stark, the sheer wilful barbarity of the scene tells us something vital about the story Martin is telling: in this world, no one is safe.

In Westeros, the law of guest right is one of the few sacred rules that is shared by followers of all religions, from Northern lords like the Old Bear, Jeor Mormont of the Night's Watch ('there is no crime so foul as for a guest to bring murder into a man's hall'),[3] to Prince Doran Martell of Dorne ('Ser Balon is a guest beneath my roof. He has eaten of my bread and salt. I will not do him harm'[4]). At the Red Wedding, that law is broken in spectacular fashion – a sign not just of the merciless nature of Lord Walder Frey and his collaborators, Tywin Lannister and Roose Bolton, but of the overall moral degeneracy poisoning the Seven Kingdoms.

In the real world, unwritten laws of guest right go all the way back to Ancient Greece, to whom the right of xenia (meaning stranger), or in Latin hospitium, was every bit as sacred as it is in Westeros. Guests were said to be watched over by Zeus, who in his role as protector of strangers and supplicants would take on the name Zeus Xenios, the patron of hospitality. Several Greek myths revolve around the appearance of a mysterious stranger who, having received kind treatment from a generous host, reveals him or herself as a divine entity, and bestows favours upon the host in turn: 'the moral is to treat every guest as a disguised god ... be a generous host to every guest, regardless of social status.'[5]

But the rules of *xenia* didn't just apply to hosts: guests, too, were expected to behave appropriately, to 'show respect by not overeating at the host's table, giving sincere thanks, sharing stories and news, and expanding the host's good reputation by telling others of [their] generosity and kindness'.[6] Indeed, the entire Trojan conflict was sparked by a particularly flagrant breach of *xenia*, as Priam of Troy falls madly in love with Helen, the wife of his host, Menelaus of Sparta, and abducts her, forcing the Greeks to declare war.

A similar incident occurs in the histories behind *A Song of Ice and Fire*, as Lyanna Stark, then betrothed to Robert Baratheon, is seemingly snatched away by the heir to the throne, Rhaegar Targaryen. This transgression is mitigated by the fact that neither the Starks nor the Baratheons were hosting Rhaegar at the time – the abduction happened on the road to Harrenhal – but it nonetheless sparks a major conflagration, and the downfall of Rhaegar's dynasty.

By the medieval period, laws of guest right were not so clearly defined, with differing codes and customs across countries and regions, while much of the work of providing succour to travellers and refugees was now taken

Sudden death: Catelyn
Stark (Michelle Fairley)
is murdered by Black
Walder (Tim Plester)
at the Red Wedding

# 'The laws of hospitality are as old as the first men, and sacred as a heart tree'

Mance Rayder, *A Storm of Swords*[7]

up by monastic orders. However, ideas of hospitality were still 'a prominent feature of early medieval law ... hosts [were] expected to protect their guests'.[8] Which explains the outrage that greeted a pair of incidents in medieval Scotland, both of which directly inspired the Red Wedding.

As part of an audio guide launched in 2020, visitors to Edinburgh Castle can hear the voice of George R.R. Martin informing them just how much of his work was drawn from local events:

> Scottish history is amazingly bloody and dark and twisted and full of betrayals and battles. The Red Wedding ... was inspired in large part by two events in Scottish history – the Black Dinner here in Edinburgh ... and the Glencoe Massacre, when the Campbells slaughtered the MacDonalds. I combined the two of those and threw in a wedding and you get the Red Wedding.[9]

At the Black Dinner of 1440, 15-year-old William Douglas, recently named the Sixth Earl of Douglas, was invited to Edinburgh Castle along with his younger brother at the behest of King James II of Scotland – himself a child of 10. Following the meal, the severed head of a black bull was thrown onto the table, at which point

the young Douglases were dragged off, tried on dubious charges and beheaded. As with the Red Wedding, however, the apparent host of the event was acting on someone else's orders – though historians still argue over who exactly was behind the plot. Many point fingers at the Tywin-esque figure of Lord Chancellor William Crichton, whose supporters conducted the mock trial. Others, however, accuse members of the boys' own family, specifically their great-uncle, 'known to posterity as James the Gross for his tedious inaction and corpulence'.[10] According to historian David C. Weinczok in his book on the Scottish history that underpins Martin's work, James 'reaped a considerable boon from the Black Dinner, becoming the Seventh Earl of Douglas and head of the Black Douglas family in the wake of the murder of his grand-nephews – something that would never have happened if either William or David had lived to produce an heir.'[11] We should also note that James's insulting epithet was also borrowed for *A Song of Ice and Fire*, wherein we hear of (but have yet to meet) a Tyrell family member known to all as Garth the Gross, apparently due to his excessive flatulence.

The second event to inspire the Red Wedding was even bloodier. The two Highland clans at the centre of the Glencoe Massacre – the MacDonalds and the Campbells – had a long history of feuding. By 1692 that enmity had taken on a political dimension, as the MacDonalds continued to support the ousted King James and his Jacobite uprising while the Campbells put their weight behind the new monarchs, William III and Mary II. As government authorities began to put pressure on clans like the MacDonalds to swear allegiance to the new royal family, around 120 soldiers under the command of Captain Robert Campbell were dispatched to the Highland town of Glencoe, where they were given bed and board by the MacDonalds. On the morning of 13 February, however, the soldiers rose up and began to slaughter their hosts, killing some 38 men, women and children and driving many more out into the mountains where they died from exposure.

**TOP**
A place of infamy: Edinburgh Castle, site of the infamous Black Dinner of 1440

**BOTTOM**
A betrayal of guest right: *The Abduction of Helen*, a seventeenth-century painting by Frans Francken the Younger

**ABOVE**
Flight into the
wilderness: the 1889
artwork *After the
Massacre of Glencoe*
by Peter Graham

**OPPOSITE**
Bonny Scotland:
a bucolic view of
the real Glencoe,
in the heart of
the Highlands

# 'KILLING IS THE SWEETEST THING THERE IS'

The Hound, *A Clash of Kings*[12]

Though the soldiers were almost certainly acting on orders from the king or his advisors, and despite the fact that only a handful of Campbell men were involved, the massacre would nonetheless be painted as inter-clan fighting, absolving William of any responsibility. The public, however, were horrified by the events: 'at the time, when hospitality was a cornerstone of the Highlanders' way of life, this was a shocking and terrible crime.'[13] Whether the people of Westeros will end up turning against House Frey for its betrayal and murder of Robb Stark remains unclear – but there will surely be repercussions for this act of violent treachery.

Of course, this habit of knocking off beloved characters has become something of a stock-in-trade for George R.R. Martin, the inspiration behind countless memes and a source of dark humour even for the author himself. 'No one will be alive by the last book,' he told an interviewer in 1999. 'In fact, they all die in the fifth. The sixth book will be just a thousand-page description of snow blowing across the graves.'[14] But, of course, there's a serious intent behind it, too: 'Once you've accepted that you have to include death [in your stories], then you should be honest ... and indicate it can strike down anybody at any time. You don't get to live forever just because you are a cute kid or the hero's best friend or the hero.'[15]

And Martin isn't the first to kill off key characters. In 2014, at the Neuchâtel International Film Festival, the author introduced a screening of Alfred Hitchcock's *Psycho* (1960), a foundational text when it comes to unexpected deaths. '*Psycho* has tremendous impact because Janet Leigh is the movie's star,' he would tell *Rolling Stone* the same year. 'The next thing, she's being knifed in the shower. Whoever it was who said, "Kill your darlings" was referring to his favourite lines in a story, but it's just as true for characters.'[16]

And there's another, less obvious influence behind the author's penchant for surprise assassinations: Marvel Comics' The Avengers. Now a firm fixture in the cultural landscape thanks to a long-running series of summer blockbusters, this iconic superhero team were, for many years, almost exclusively the province of teenage boys and comic-book enthusiasts. For instance, the young George R.R. Martin, whose very first appearance in print was as the author of a 1964 fan letter to Avengers creators Stan Lee and Jack Kirby, published in *Fantastic Four* volume one, issue 32, and beginning 'Ho-hum! Another month, another bunch of classics, but then what can [sic] else can one expect from you chaps?'[17]

Kill your darlings: Janet Leigh comes face to face with her murderer in Alfred Hitchcock's *Psycho* (1960)

'That's all Stan Lee, and you can see it all over my work,' he would say, many years later. 'Unexpectedly killing characters, characters who are not what they seem, characters who are partly good and partly bad ... Stan Lee's fingerprints are all over that.'[19]

The world of comics would be George R.R. Martin's gateway into becoming a professional author: it was that fan letter to Lee and Kirby that, by a circuitous set of circumstances, would result in his first encounter with comic-book fanzines, allowing him to publish his fiction regularly for the first time, and to hone his craft as a storyteller. But comics would also open the floodgates for Martin not just as a reader but as a fan, the type to collect and trade issues, to discuss at great length the pros and cons of particular characters, authors and artists, and ultimately the type of fan to attend conventions, which, when Martin was young, were a relatively new and fairly obscure pastime.

The number of 'cons' that George R.R. Martin has visited since the early 1970s is impossible to count, but they gave him the opportunity to meet his heroes (and, ultimately, for his fans to meet him), while also providing him with a community, a friend group, the kind of support base that every writer needs (as well as introducing him to his wife) – none of which would've happened without the influence of Stan Lee and his unforgettable cast of characters.

As we know, Martin was a comics fan from an early age (see page 7), but it was the Fantastic Four that he really obsessed over: 'The Fantastic Four broke all the rules,' he writes in *Dreamsongs*. 'One of them was a *monster* (the Thing, who at once became my favourite), at a time when all heroes were required to be handsome.'[18] And, indeed, it's easy to see how the character of Ben Grimm – born poor, and afflicted with a hideous, rock-like physique – would appeal to the low-born, bookish, not exactly conventional-looking young Martin.

But it was a lesser-known Lee creation that would leave the deepest imprint on Martin's work. Making his debut in 1964 in *The Avengers* #9, the redeemed supervillain known as Wonder Man looked set to join regular Avengers like Ant-Man, Thor and Hulk on their upcoming adventures – until he was unexpectedly killed off in the same issue. Although Wonder Man would later be brought back, this sudden twist would shock the young Martin to his core.

**OPPOSITE**
Hero at work: Marvel legend Stan Lee with his art director John Romita in 1975

**ABOVE**
Team George: the massed ranks of *Game of Thrones* cosplayers at San Diego Comic-Con in 2016

Part Three

# WEST & SOUTH

Chapter Seven

# CASTERLY ROCK

Though as-yet unfrequented in the novels, the coastal seat of Casterly Rock – home to the conniving Lannister family – nonetheless casts a long shadow over events in *A Song of Ice and Fire*. Which is only fitting: standing over 610 m (2,000 ft) high, or three times the height of the Wall, this warren-like fortress has been built within a natural mountain of stone, rendering it all but impregnable. And again, its inspiration comes from a real source: the Rock of Gibraltar, a place George R.R. Martin had been impressed by since childhood, when he became familiar with its image in newspaper ads for Prudential Insurance. Much later, he was finally able to see it for himself. 'I visited ... and found the place just as fascinating in person as I had in print.'[1]

One of the ancient Pillars of Hercules, this limestone promontory may be smaller than Casterly Rock, but it's still colossal, rising 426 m (1,398 ft) above the Mediterranean coast with a pointed prow jutting towards the sea. And, like the Lannister seat, it is heavily fortified: the Rock of Gibraltar has been occupied since at least the eighth century, when the North African Berber chieftain, Tariq ibn-Ziyad, built the Moorish castle whose remains still stand upon it (he also gave the Rock his name – the word 'Gibraltar' is a corruption of the Arabic *Jabel-al-Tariq*, or Mountain of Tariq).

Excavations inside the Rock weren't begun until much later, however, during the eighteenth-century Great Siege of Gibraltar, during which Spanish and French forces tried to wrest control of the Rock and its surrounding country from the occupying British. Over the years, more and more tunnels were excavated, and the Rock now contains '[55 km] (34 miles) of tunnels, more than 150 halls, chambers, and caves, Napoleonic gunports and cannons looking out over land and sea, stalagmites and stalactites, World War II bunkers, a concert hall/amphitheatre, a hospital (WWII era), and ancient mines'.[2] No wonder Martin is still planning to include Casterly Rock in later instalments, 'so I can show you

all the wonders and terrors and treasures of House Lannister first hand'.[3]

Of course, Casterly Rock is most renowned for two major exports: gold and ambition. The first of these is sourced from mines deep beneath the Rock and is so plentiful that there is an entire room within the keep – the Golden Gallery – whose walls are made of the stuff.[4] Since his accession, Tywin Lannister has used this wealth to further his family's ambitions, until the day when his son is Lord Commander of the Kingsguard, his daughter Queen of the Seven Kingdoms, and both his grandsons (officially named Baratheon, but actually Lannisters through both incestuous parents) inherit the Iron Throne, with himself as Hand of the King.

Not that any of this seems to make Tywin particularly happy. Indeed, for all their achievements, the Lannister brood are a constant disappointment to their patriarch, none more so than Tywin's youngest son, Tyrion, the sharp-tongued, priapic dwarf who Martin has claimed – repeatedly – is his most beloved character in the series ('Tyrion is my favorite character. Okay? OKAY? Can we PLEASE put that one to rest??'[5]). He has also suggested that if fans 'looked hard enough'[6] they might find parallels between Tyrion and that other paragon of political cunning, Richard III: both are the youngest sons

Rock of ages: Gibraltar in reality (top) and as GRRM first encountered it, in a long-running series of Prudential insurance ads (bottom)

'All dwarves are bastards
in their father's eyes':
Tyrion Lannister (Peter
Dinklage, left) and his
villainous patriarch,
Tywin (Charles Dance)
in *Game of Thrones*

# 'THERE IS NO LIMIT TO LANNISTER PRIDE'

Catelyn Stark, *A Game of Thrones*[7]

'Never forget what you are,
for surely the world will not.
Make it your strength. Then
it can never be your weakness.
Armor yourself in it, and it will
never be used to hurt you.'

Tyrion Lannister, *A Game of Thrones*[8]

of powerful men, after all, and both are beset by physical challenges. And both seem more at home behind a desk than on the battlefield: Tyrion's installation as Hand sees him take charge of the king's bickering small council, while even 'the most cynical critics will concede Richard did good work as the first Lord President of the Council of the North in Yorkshire'.[9]

But perhaps the clearest parallel between Richard and Tyrion is in how the rest of the world sees them. While the public perception of Richard III is as a scheming villain, the bent-backed murderer of the Princes in the Tower from Shakespeare's great tragedy, many modern historians have come to doubt this depiction, which became widespread during the reign of Richard's adversary, Henry VII, and his descendants. Similarly, while Tyrion works to improve the lot of everyone in King's Landing – shoring up the city's defences, appointing a new Commander of the City Watch, curbing his royal nephew's more outrageous behaviour – he is nonetheless treated as a pariah, a 'twisted little monkey demon'[10]

blamed for all the worst excesses of his family. For George R.R. Martin, Tyrion is 'who I want to be':[11] wise, diplomatic, razor-sharp and swift with a put-down, but also deeply emotional, empathetic, and able to see right to the truth of things.

But that's not all Tyrion is. It cannot be overlooked that he's also a murderer – not just of his father, Tywin, whom most would agree had it coming, but also of his former lover, the 'camp follower' Shae. True, she had betrayed him in the worst imaginable fashion – delivering cruel, mocking evidence against him in court before jumping into bed with the very father who despises him – but Tyrion still strangles her, throttling the life out of her with his father's chain of office, after recalling in graphic detail all the times they made love.

Shae isn't the first woman to die in *A Song of Ice and Fire*, and she certainly won't be the last. She's not the first to be treated as an object by powerful men, bought and sold for their pleasure, and she's not the first to be depicted as ruthlessly ambitious, willing to betray the man who professes to love her. But she is the first to be murdered by a character that we've been strongly encouraged to identify with, and her death raises questions about the nature of violence both in *A Song of Ice and Fire* and its small-screen adaptation, and particularly violence against women.

From its very first episode, HBO's *Game of Thrones* didn't shy away from depicting sexualized violence, as the teenage Daenerys Targaryen is raped by her husband, Khal Drogo – a scene that, in fact, plays out very differently in the book, wherein Daenerys is, at least on this first night, a willing participant.[12] But there is nonetheless plenty of sexual violence in *A Song of Ice and Fire* – one online analysis counts no less than 214 examples of rape, either depicted or reported, over the course of the five books, from Craster's abuse of his daughters to the widespread rape committed by the Dothraki[13] – and, some of it, like the violation of Jeyne Poole by Ramsay Bolton in *A Dance With Dragons*, is extremely detailed and disturbing.

The crooked king: Laurence Olivier as Richard III in his 1956 film version of Shakespeare's play

# 'FOR HANDS OF GOLD ARE ALWAYS COLD, BUT A WOMAN'S HANDS ARE WARM'

Tongue, *A Storm of Swords*[14]

For Martin, the explicit nature of this violence is precisely the point. 'Rape and sexual violence have been a part of every war ever fought, from the ancient Sumerians to our present day,' he told the *New York Times* in 2014:

> To omit them from a narrative centred on war and power would have been fundamentally false and dishonest, and would have undermined one of the themes of the books: that the true horrors of human history derive not from orcs and Dark Lords, but from ourselves ... Whatever might be happening in my books, I try to put the reader into the middle of it ... Certain scenes are *meant* to be uncomfortable, disturbing, hard to read.[15]

For some commentators, however, this justification isn't fully convincing. They point to the fact that, however much Martin's books may be inspired by real history, they are still essentially fantasy stories: if the reader is able to accept the presence of dragons, perhaps they'd also accept a little less sexual violence. They also point out that such violence is almost exclusively committed against women, despite the fact that male-on-male rape was not uncommon in the medieval period, and that the books contain a number of all-male organizations, such as the Night's Watch. As blogger RibaldRemark writes: 'Martin's work suggests that it is more believable that an army of men, made up of the dregs of humanity ... don't indulge in rape, whereas the rape of noblewomen, protected female wards and commoners alike is commonplace.'[16] It should be noted that sexual violence against men is not entirely unknown in the books – there's the genital mutilation of poor Theon Greyjoy, while in *A Dance With Dragons* we learn that the Ironborn captive Maester Kerwin has been 'dragged ... belowdecks and used ... as a woman'[17] – but these are drops beside the ocean of violent incidents involving female characters.

The controversy around sexual violence in *Game of Thrones* would blow up in 2014, when the troubling but essentially consensual sex scene Martin wrote between Cersei and Jaime in the Great Sept beside the body of their dead son became, in HBO's adaptation, an act of forced coupling (the rape of Sansa Stark in Season Five would only fan the flames). The resulting outcry – which tied into the burgeoning online #metoo movement – would force showrunners David Benioff and D.B. Weiss into the uncomfortable position of having to justify the depiction of sex and violence in the series, while at

Seduction and betrayal: Tyrion Lannister (Peter Dinklage) with his doomed lover Shae (Sibel Kekilli) in *Game of Thrones* (top); and Prince Daemon Targaryen (Matt Smith) with his niece and future wife Princess Rhaenyra (Milly Alcock) in *House of the Dragon* (bottom)

the same time claiming that 'not one word of the scripts ... have been changed in any way, shape or form by what people said on the Internet, or elsewhere'.[18]

However, their claim would seem to be undermined by the fact that later seasons of *Game of Thrones* featured a noticeable drop-off in on-screen rape – a tonal shift that has thus far been carried over into *House of the Dragon,* which, unlike *Game of Thrones,* has employed multiple female directors. While the spin-off series does still depict in graphic detail the sufferings of women, these tend to be in the birthing bed rather than at the hands of predatory men – though whether future volumes in Martin's book series will see a similar downplaying of sexual violence remains to be seen.

Of course, the depiction of women in *A Song of Ice and Fire* doesn't exclusively involve sexual assault and suffering. 'I wanted to present my female characters in great diversity,' Martin told an interviewer in 2012. 'Even in a society as sexist and patriarchal as the Seven Kingdoms of Westeros ... women with different talents would find ways to work within society, according to who they are.'

And indeed, the female characters in Martin's work are just as complex and many-faceted as the men. There's Olenna Tyrell, the 'Queen of Thorns', who exercises a quiet but implacable power, masterminding the murder of Joffrey Baratheon and manipulating the outcome of the war for her own ends (though she is outwitted by Tywin Lannister, who steals Sansa Stark from under her nose by marrying her to his son Tyrion). There's Catelyn Stark, whose maternal instincts can drive her to be both protective and callous, as she admits when discussing her treatment of the young Jon Snow. And, of course, there's the equally zealous Cersei Lannister, whose ruthless ambition and preening self-image as a 'lioness' are somewhat undermined by the fact that she's not nearly as clever as she thinks she is.

Then there are two extraordinary warrior women, separated by geography but united by their skill and ferocity on the battlefield: Brienne of Tarth and Asha Greyjoy (renamed Yara in the HBO series, presumably to avoid confusion with another resilient woman, the loyal Wildling, Osha). Perhaps surprisingly, given the era's fierce misogyny, both these women have notable medieval antecedents.

For Asha's inspiration, we might look no further than Freydís Eiríksdóttir, child of the Norse adventurer Erik the Red and sister of Leif Erikson, reportedly the first European to make contact with the tribes of Vinland, or North America. As portrayed in a pair of Icelandic sagas – the *Saga of the Greenlanders* and the *Saga of Erik the Red* – Freydís is an ambitious woman who travels to Vinland in search of her own independent wealth. In the latter saga she's also depicted as a ruthless warrior, rallying the Vikings when their camp is attacked at night by bands of *Skrælingar,* or Native Americans. At three months pregnant, Freydís picks up the sword of a fallen comrade, 'let down her sark (or garment) and struck her breast with the naked sword. At this they were frightened, and rushed off to their boats'.[19] Martin may 'no longer recall the titles'[20] of the Icelandic sagas he read at college, but it would seem that some of the characters may have lingered in his memory.

But if Asha is a fairly straightforward warrior woman, given to drinking, fighting and reaving in the finest Ironborn tradition, her counterpart, Brienne, is a more complex and modern character, powerfully strong and skilled with weapons, but also racked with self-doubt and insecurity. Perhaps the most straightforwardly decent character in the entire story, Brienne has, like Sansa Stark, grown up with tales of chivalry and valour, only to find that the real world is a much less forgiving place than it appears in the stories. Unlike Sansa, however, Brienne grew up identifying not with the damsels in those tales but with the knights themselves, dreaming from an early age of winning her spurs and becoming a warrior. The discovery that the majority of these knights are either bullies, brutes or cowards hasn't swayed her – Brienne yearns for glory, and her happiest moment comes when Renly Baratheon names her to his Rainbow Guard: 'her smile lit up her face, and her voice was strong and proud.'[21]

Land ho! The Vikings sight Vineland in the 1893 artwork *Leiv Eiriksson Discovering America* by Christian Krohg

## 'You have courage. Not battle courage, perhaps, but ... a kind of *woman's* courage'

Brienne of Tarth, *A Clash of Kings*[22]

Real-world antecedents for Brienne are hard to pinpoint: the most ruthless women of ancient times tended to be queens, like the Celtic revolutionary Boudicca or the Syrian conqueror Zenobia, rather than battlefield knights. So medieval scholars point instead to a pair of fictional heroines, or rather one woman under two names: Bradamante, heroine of the Italian romances *Orlando Innamorato* (1495) by Matteo Maria Boiardo and *Orlando Furioso* (1516) by Ludovico Ariosto, and her English equivalent, Britomart, from Edmund Spenser's epic poem *The Faerie Queen*, written in the 1590s.[23]

Like Brienne, Bradamante is a proficient warrior, serving the Emperor Charlemagne as he fights to repel an invasion of Saracens into France. Unlike Brienne, however, she carries a magic lance and has a committed paramour: the rogue Saracen Ruggiero, whom she rescues from the clutches of a powerful wizard. Britomart, meanwhile, is a wandering knight sworn to no particular lord, and, like Brienne, she is a virgin, symbolizing the virtue of chastity.[24] But Britomart also carries a charmed weapon – in this case, a magical spear – and she also has a beloved: Artegall, the Knight of Justice. But, perhaps most importantly, she – like Bradamante before her – is also very beautiful, a paragon of virtuous youth,

rather than the lumbering, inelegant Brienne, who, with her broken nose, prominent teeth and hair like 'a squirrel's nest of dirty straw',[25] is only named The Beauty in mockery.

Fantasy literature has, of course, traditionally struggled to include women: the genre's greatest work, *The Lord of the Rings*, famously contains just a handful of female characters, who appear only intermittently. By placing female characters at the heart of his invented world, George R.R. Martin is perhaps attempting to right some of the wrongs of the past, while also offering readers of both sexes a more inclusive set of heroes and villains. In the modern cultural landscape, writing female characters can be something of a minefield for a male author – but it's one that Martin is clearly committed to navigating.

**ABOVE**
The female knight Britomart from Spenser's *The Faerie Queene*, as illustrated by Walter Crane in 1896

**OPPOSITE**
Blade of a warrior: Brienne (Gwendoline Christie) unsheathes her sword Oathkeeper in *Game of Thrones*

Chapter Eight

# HIGHGARDEN AND THE REACH

In 1314, at the court of King Philip IV of France, three noblewomen were tried for the very serious crime of adultery. Their names were Margaret of Burgundy, Blanche of Burgundy and Joan II, Countess of Burgundy, and they were all three married to the king's sons: Louis, Philip and Charles. The charges against them were simple: that all three had been regularly slipping off to a nearby guard tower, the Tour de Nesle, to drink and commit carnal sins with two brothers, Walter and Philip of Aunay.

At their trial, Margaret and Blanche were found guilty; their heads were shaved and they were sentenced to life in prison, where Margaret would die in suspicious circumstances (Blanche was lucky enough to end her life in a nunnery). Meanwhile, the Aunay brothers were caught trying to escape to England and were tortured,

tried, castrated and executed. But how did they come to be accused in the first place?

While the facts of the case will never be known, historians – and authors like George R.R. Martin's beloved Maurice Druon, who fictionalized the affair in his *Accursed Kings* series (1955–77) – have singled out one likely source for the rumours: the accused women's sister-in-law, Isabella, known as the She-Wolf of France. At the time, Isabella was married to Edward II of England, and though their marriage was far from a happy one, at the time of the affair Isabella was pregnant with Edward's child and may have been seeking a way for her son to claim the thrones of both England and France (and also to distract from rumours about her own liaison with the English nobleman Roger Mortimer). Either way, the incident that would come to be known as the Tour de Nesle Affair fatally weakened the French monarchy, leading – upon the death of Philip IV – to a succession crisis and ultimately to the Hundred Years War.

More than two centuries later, on 2 May 1536, the wife of King Henry VIII, Anne Boleyn, was arrested and taken to the Tower of London on similar but even more extreme charges: adultery, incest and high treason. Implicated alongside her were: several courtiers; a Flemish

musician named Mark Smeaton, who had confessed to an affair with the queen, but possibly under torture; and Anne's own brother, George Boleyn, who stood accused of two incidents of incestuous behaviour with his sister. George, Smeaton and three others would be executed on 17 May; Anne would follow on 19 May, opening the way for Henry to marry his new love, Jane Seymour. This time, the finger has been pointed at the king's chief minister, Thomas Cromwell, with one contemporary observer claiming that, on the orders of the king, Cromwell 'set himself to devise and conspire the said affair'.[1]

For readers of *A Song of Ice and Fire*, the parallels between these historical incidents and the events depicted in *A Feast for Crows* are inescapable. In that book, an increasingly paranoid Cersei Lannister attempts to do away with her troublesome daughter-in-law, Margaery Tyrell, by spreading rumours of the younger queen's adultery, first with a singer named the Blue Bard – who, like Smeaton, is tortured for his confession – and then with several knights, including Ser Osney Kettleblack, whom Cersei has herself seduced. Margaery is arrested with two of her cousins and imprisoned by the High Sparrow, while Cersei does her best to further blacken the younger woman's name.

**TOP**
Accursed king: Philip le Bel of France and his troublesome family in an illustration from 1313

**BOTTOM**
An inconvenient woman: the execution of Anne Boleyn, from a seventeenth-century German engraving

**OVERLEAF**
'Shame... Shame... Shame...': Cersei Lannister (Lena Headey) takes her walk of atonement through King's Landing in *Game of Thrones*

But, despite her unflinching belief in her own cunning, Cersei doesn't, in fact, possess the wiles of an Isabella or a Thomas Cromwell. Ultimately, her accusations will rebound in spectacular fashion, leading to her own arrest and imprisonment, and finally her demeaning walk of shame through the streets of King's Landing. Once again, we see George R.R. Martin taking inspiration from real incidents, twisting them together and tugging them apart, exploring some of the other ways that events might have played out if the circumstances had been different.

Queen Margaery is, of course, a daughter of Highgarden, another castle that, like Casterly Rock, has yet to make an appearance in the books, but whose wealth and reputation precede it. For the Tyrells, their affluence derives not from gold but from grain: their kingdom of the Reach is known to be the most fertile in all Westeros, while Highgarden itself has 'fields of golden roses that stretch away as far as the eye can see. The fruits are so ripe they explode in your mouth – melons, peaches, fireplums, you've never tasted such sweetness'.[3]

Highgarden is also the chivalric heart of Westeros, a place where the old heroic tales are taken most seriously and where youth and beauty are prized above all else. In *A Clash of Kings*, the warriors of the Reach are dubbed by Catelyn Stark as the knights of summer: 'all they see is the chance for glory and honour and spoils. They are boys drunk on song and story, and like all boys, they think themselves immortal.'[4]

In Catelyn's words, we might detect the ghostly impression of another of George R.R. Martin's favourite books: an unforgettable story of glamorous youth in a decadent age. First encountered by Martin at an impressionable time – 'in my early twenties, when I was just coming off the sad ending of the first great love of my life'[5] – F. Scott Fitzgerald's *The Great Gatsby* (1925) is another of the novels chosen by the author as one of his five favourites in any genre.[6]

Told through the eyes of a First World War veteran named Nick Carraway and

## 'The world was simpler in those times ... and men as well as swords were made of finer steel'

Thoughts of Jaime Lannister, *A Storm of Swords*[2]

set amid the wealthy estates of Long Island in 1922, Fitzgerald's novel traces the obsessive efforts of Carraway's neighbour, Jay Gatsby, to reclaim the love of his life, Daisy Buchanan. Often hailed as the greatest of all American novels, the book is richly nostalgic, concerned with 'the impossibilities of recapturing the past, the role of myths in our lives, the shattered dreams of our youth'.[7]

The influence of *The Great Gatsby* might be detected in the self-deluding, ultimately rather pathetic yearning felt by Petyr Baelish for his childhood paramour, Catelyn Stark, for whose sake he is willing to scheme, betray and even murder – though never, of course, with his own hands. 'For Gatsby,' Martin would tell PBS's *Great American Read* series, his obsession with Daisy 'was a bittersweet journey, and a doomed pursuit'[8] – much like Littlefinger's.

But Fitzgerald's impact is most powerfully felt in Martin's depiction of those young knights of Highgarden, a band of carefree innocents who will soon come face to face with brutal reality. As Catelyn says: 'War will make them old ... They are the knights of summer, and winter is coming.'[9]

Further south, on the coast of the Reach, we arrive at another location that looms large both literally and figuratively

**LEFT**
Onward, Christian soldiers: Jan Van Eyck's Knights of Christ from *The Ghent Altarpiece*, 1432

**RIGHT**
Author F. Scott Fitzgerald photographed in 1920 (bottom), five years before the publication of his masterpiece, *The Great Gatsby* (first edition, top)

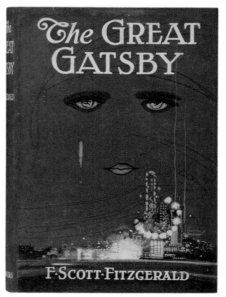

The Ale House

# 'Sorcery is a sword without a hilt. There is no safe way to grasp it.'

Dalla, *A Storm of Swords*[10]

in *A Song of Ice and Fire*, though it has thus far appeared only fleetingly in the story. The city of Oldtown, with its great spire, the Hightower, is the largest and wealthiest metropolis in Westeros; King's Landing may have more inhabitants, but the majority of these are crammed into slums and shanty towns. Oldtown is too proud to permit such indigence: this is a city built on trade, learning and reputation – and, as we see in *House of the Dragon*, its lords, the Hightowers, were once second only to the Targaryens in wealth and influence.

Described as 'a veritable labyrinth of a city, all wynds and crisscrossing alleys and narrow crookback streets',[11] Oldtown's stone buildings and cobbled streets feel more modern than the staunchly medieval King's Landing. Home both to the Citadel, where maesters are trained to carry out their duties, and the Starry Sept, the heart of religion in Westeros before the building of the Sept of Baelor, Oldtown carries strong echoes of English university towns like Oxford and Cambridge – and, indeed, Martin's description of Oldtown 'emerging ghostlike from the predawn gloom' to reveal 'the domes and towers of the Citadel'[12] are a short step from the poet Matthew Arnold's famous nineteenth-century description of Oxford: 'That sweet city with her dreaming spires.'[13] Fittingly, the handful of Oldtown residents that

we're introduced to in the Prologue to *A Feast for Crows* are almost all students, maesters in training who spend their days in study and their evenings drinking at the Quill and Tankard, an alehouse straight out of Charles Dickens.

The maesters themselves have no single historical equivalent: rather they are a combination of many roles, from monks, alchemists and healers to scribes, record keepers and even postmen, for it is the maester's job to keep the ravens fed and caged. There is also, perhaps, just the faintest whiff of wizardry about them, though any dabbling with the 'dark arts' is severely frowned upon by the Citadel's conclave, and liable to result in the maester in question being stripped of his chain. Not that such threats stop every curious maester from seeking out such forbidden lore, and even profiting from it. As the terrifying Maester Qyburn says, 'The Citadel took my chain, but they could not take my knowledge',[14] as he proves when he introduces the monstrous Ser Robert Strong, a giant of a knight who does not speak and bears a suspicious similarity to the recently deceased Gregor Clegane, a.k.a. the Mountain.

But, while it may have the power to resurrect the dead, predict the future and open doorways to other realms, magic is not a common element in *A Song of Ice and Fire*, and this is entirely intentional. 'Fantasy needs magic in it,' Martin said in 2017, 'but I try to control the magic very strictly. You can have too much magic … and you lose all sense of realism.' Mentioning no names, he also took aim at those fantasy franchises that make magic appear easy and non-threatening. 'I try to keep the magic magical – something mysterious and dark and dangerous, and something never completely understood. I don't want to go down the route of having magic schools and classes where, if you say these six words, something will reliably happen. Magic doesn't work that way.'[15] Once again, we can detect the influence of Ursula Le Guin, in whose work magic is seen as something challenging and dangerous, to be used only by those with the skill and temperament to do so.

**TOP**
'Dreaming spires':
The stone cloisters of
the English university
town, Oxford

**BOTTOM**
Drink and be merry:
1832 illustration *The
Ale House* by George
Cruikshank

'A MIND NEEDS BOOKS
LIKE A SWORD NEEDS
A WHETSTONE'

Tyrion Lannister, *A Game of Thrones*[16]

Halls of learning:
an 1870 woodcut
depicting the lost
Library of Alexandria
by O. Von Corven

As she writes in *A Wizard of Earthsea*: 'need alone is not enough to set power free: there must be knowledge.'[17]

And knowledge is something that the educated citizens of Oldtown pride themselves on: indeed, one characteristic that the Citadel does share with fantasy's many schools of magic, from the School for Wizards in the *Earthsea* series to J.K. Rowling's Hogwarts and Terry Pratchett's Unseen University, is its enormous library. From rare histories of Old Valyria to arcane works on the care and breeding of dragons, from the doings of the Targaryen kings to ballads that date back before the coming of the Andals, the Citadel's collection of books is by far the largest in Westeros.

Its closest historical comparison, then, must be the great Library of Alexandria in Egypt, which, at its height, was said to have housed anywhere from 40,000 to 400,000 scrolls on every conceivable topic and from every part of the world. Though the city itself was founded by the Macedonian general, Alexander the Great – one of many he ordered to be built during his conquests – plans for the library were begun either by Alexander's friend, historian and bodyguard, Ptolemy I, or by his son, Ptolemy II. The dynasty that Ptolemy founded would reign over Egypt for almost three centuries following Alexander's death in 323 BC, and the library would thrive under its guardianship, drawing scholars, poets and historians from across the civilized world. Sadly, it could not survive indefinitely – part of the library was burned during the civil wars instigated by Julius Caesar in 48 BC, and the rest was probably destroyed some three centuries later during an invasion by Queen Zenobia of Palmyra. But, while it lasted, the Library of Alexandria was, like the Citadel, 'the greatest repository of knowledge in the known world'.[18]

Of course, the knowledge of the Citadel is contained not in papyrus scrolls, but in hard-bound books. 'There are so many books at the Citadel that no man can hope to read them all,'[19] Jon Snow tells Sam Tarly – a surefire way to get his friend's attention, given that Sam is, along with Tyrion Lannister, the most voracious reader in *A Song of Ice and Fire*. Not coincidentally, he's also the nearest thing *A Song of Ice and Fire* has to a 'self-insert' character: the one who most resembles his creator, in outlook and temperament if not in age or appearance. As Martin said in 2017: 'The character I'm probably most like in real life is Samwell Tarly. Good old Sam!'[20]

Of course, Sam is also just one in a long line of fictional heroes whose greatest love is the study of books. From Elizabeth Bennet in *Pride and Prejudice* (1813) – 'she is a great reader, and has no pleasure in anything else'[21] – via Holden Caulfield in *The Catcher in the Rye* (1951) – 'I'm quite illiterate, but I read a lot'[22] – to Guy Montag in *Fahrenheit 451* (1953) , whose desire to read leaves him an exile from his wife, his workmates and ultimately his entire society, the heroes of great literary works are often readers themselves (largely, one suspects, because their authors are). For someone who adores reading as much as George R.R. Martin, it was inevitable that this passion would end up seeping through into his characters.

**TOP**
A pair of bookworms: Elizabeth Bennet (Jennifer Ehle, left) in the BBC's *Pride and Prejudice* (1995); and Guy Montag (Oskar Werner, right) with his flamethrower in the 1966 film *Fahrenheit 451*

**BOTTOM**
Quill and parchment: Sam (John Bradley) and Gilly (Hannah Murray) study their history in *Game of Thrones*

# Chapter Nine
# DORNE

When the producers of HBO's *Game of Thrones* began scouting locations to represent the southernmost kingdom of Westeros, there was only one real contender. From its food (bold and spicy) to its people (much the same), Dorne is quite different from the rest of the continent: as the stray Kingsguard knight Ser Arys Oakheart reflects: 'men said it was the food that made Dornishmen so hot-tempered and their women so wild and wanton. Fiery peppers and strange spices heat the blood.'[1] The model, then, is obviously Spain. As we've learned, George R.R. Martin is no stranger to this country: he has visited on numerous occasions and is happy to admit that these trips played a key role in his conception of Dorne: 'I always pictured the Martells ... as Mediterraneans.'[2]

Many of the Dorne scenes in *Game of Thrones* were filmed in the flowering gardens of the Alcázar de Sevilla in Spain

But Dorne's distinctiveness isn't merely the result of geography. From the histories of Westeros, we learn that several centuries before the coming of the Targaryen kings, parts of Dorne were invaded and settled by the Rhoynar, river-dwellers from Essos who had been driven from their homes following a war with the Valyrian Empire. Led by the legendary Queen Nymeria, these newcomers made an alliance with House Martell of Dorne, uniting their two peoples under a banner displaying both the Rhoynish sun and the Martell spear.

The Rhoynish influence can be detected in Dorne's architecture, its food and its sense of itself as a kingdom apart from the other six. 'Dorne is a very special land, with a slightly different cultural basis than the rest of Westeros,' Martin told a Spanish interviewer in 2012. 'It was politically apart for a long time, it was also culturally apart because of the Rhoynar and the traditions they brought ... I see that in Spain ... particularly the Moorish history of Spain.'[3]

The first notable Dornishman that we meet in *A Song of Ice and Fire* is also, thus far, the most iconic: Oberyn Martell, the silver-tongued princeling played in the HBO series by Chilean-born actor, Pedro Pascal. Introduced by Martin in *A Storm of Swords*, Oberyn is a prime example of the coast-dwelling 'salty' Dornishmen of the extreme south: 'lithe and dark, with smooth olive skin and long black hair streaming in the wind.'[4] In his behaviour, too, Oberyn fits not just the Westerosi caricature of a Dornishman – he lives a life of pleasure, has fathered no less than eight bastard girls and is utterly reckless in combat – but also the old-fashioned stereotype of the cocky Spaniard as found in everything from the novels of Ernest Hemingway to the movie *Puss in Boots* (2011). And the mantra he repeats when he comes to fight Ser Gregor Clegane – 'you raped her, you murdered her, you killed her children'[5] – must surely have been inspired by the oft-quoted line uttered by the moustache-twirling Spanish swordsman in William Goldman's fantasy pastiche *The Princess Bride* (1987): 'Hello. My name is Inigo Montoya. You killed my father. Prepare to die.'[6]

Martin's second major influence for Dorne, however, would seem almost the precise opposite of the first. 'Dorne is definitely influenced a bit by Spain,' Martin has said, '(but also) a bit by Wales.'[7] So how did this dramatic but rather damp corner of the British Isles come to inspire the desert lands of southern Westeros?

Along the border between Wales and England lie the Welsh Marches, an area of land whose precise geographical definition

# 'YOU WILL NOT BEND US, BREAK US, OR MAKE US BOW. THIS IS DORNE.'

Meria Martell, *The World of Ice and Fire*[8]

# 'No true man killed with poison ... Poison was for cravens, women, and Dornishmen'

Victarion Greyjoy, *A Dance With Dragons*[9]

**ABOVE**
An engraving of Owain Glyndwr depicts him seated on the Welsh throne

**OVERLEAF**
The ultimate Dornishman: Pedro Pascal smoulders as Oberyn Martell, known to his enemies as the Red Viper

has fluctuated over the centuries, but which has always been treated as a kind of demarcation zone between one land and the other. Following his invasion of England, William the Conqueror built a number of motte-and-bailey castles throughout the region, entrusting them to 'marcher lords' whose job it was to hold the line against attacks from the Welsh side. Similarly, in Westeros, we find an area of disputed borderland between Dorne and its neighbouring kingdoms referred to as the Dornish Marches, whose nobles are also known as marcher lords.

There's also the fact that both regions have a penchant for armed resistance. Just as Dorne was the only Westerosi kingdom to hold out against Aegon, fighting a series of bloody wars before it finally came under Targaryen rule almost two centuries after the Conquest, so the Welsh stood firm against William and the kings who succeeded him, before finally falling to Edward I in 1263. The Welsh were infamous for their guerilla tactics, emerging from the hills and forests to attack the English before just as quickly melting away. Similarly, as Aegon and his successors struggled to suppress Dorne, the local armies refused to meet the king in open battle, retreating to their holdfasts and striking without warning until 'the fighting degenerated

into an endless bloody series of atrocities, raids and retaliations ... murders and assassinations'.[10]

But while the Dornish may ultimately have buckled under Targaryen rule, the Welsh were not so easily cowed. In the early fifteenth century, during the reign of King Henry IV, the revolutionary Owain Glyndwr proclaimed himself Prince of Wales, sparking a conflict that would last for more than a decade. Seizing control of numerous strongholds, including the mighty Harlech Castle, Glyndwr's rulership over his newly independent Wales was recognized and legitimized by several European nations, including France and Spain – but, again, it couldn't last. Though Glyndwr himself was never officially killed or captured, English rule was returned to Wales in 1415, and for decades afterwards Welshmen would be forbidden to hold lands or serve on juries, or even to marry English brides.

But while the Dornish may be renowned for their stamina in battle, they are also known to employ more devious methods of waging war – indeed, Oberyn Martell is so notorious for his use of a poisoned blade that he has earned the nickname the Red Viper. In the real world, the use of poison as a weapon dates back to the very earliest human civilizations: archaeologists have found evidence of primitive weapons containing hidden grooves that are believed to have been used to store poison, while ancient Mesopotamian texts dating from as far back as 4,500 BC tell of a 'poison not curable'.[11] The early Egyptian king Menes was said to have studied poisonous plants, while the Roman emperor Claudius was rumoured to have been poisoned by his wife, Agrippina. His successor, Nero, even employed his own personal poisoner, the Gaulish woman, Locusta, whom he allegedly dispatched against several members of his family.

The appeal of poison is self-evident: here is a weapon that leaves little or no evidence and, if employed carefully, cannot be traced back to the wielder. Poisoning would become particularly popular during the medieval period, thanks to an increase in the availability of medicinal herbs and supplies, many

of which could be used to harm as well as cure. These would be sold in apothecaries, shops that catered not just to healers and medics but also to the general public.

Among those of royal blood alleged to have been poisoned in the medieval period are: King John of England, a spiteful character whose name lives on in the legends of Robin Hood; Anne Neville, Queen of England and the wife of Richard III, who was said to have murdered her; and Catherine of Aragon, the first wife of Henry VIII, whom he divorced to marry Anne Boleyn, but whose continued existence was a thorn in Henry's side. Whether any of these rumours are true remains in doubt, but that is irrelevant: tales of royal poisoning were rife in the medieval period and crop up frequently both in true and fictionalized histories of the period.

Among the most popular medieval poisons were hemlock, a plant used to treat swollen joints, but which in larger quantities could cause paralysis and asphyxiation; and aconite or wolfsbane, a poison used to bait animals, but which can also cause heart failure in humans. In the same period, Middle Eastern apothecaries became skilled in the creation of arsenic: 'the first reliable and lethal poison that was odourless, tasteless and colourless and would work in powder, solution or gaseous form'.[12]

Arsenic is clearly the inspiration for the poison known as the Tears of Lys, a tasteless and undetectable killer brewed by the alchemists of that eastern city, and almost certainly used by Lysa Arryn[13] to murder her husband, the King's Hand, on the orders of Petyr Baelish. Other poisons known to be utilized in Westeros are nightshade – presumably the sap of the belladonna plant, known to us as deadly nightshade – various mushrooms and toadstools, such as greycap, and venoms extracted from lizards and snakes. The deadliest Westerosi poison – a substance known only as the Strangler and used to murder King Joffrey – would seem to have been inspired by strychnine, a poison that causes violent convulsions and ultimately asphyxiation. Though not common in medieval Europe, it has been used for centuries in India, home to the *Strychnos nux-vomica* plant from which the poison is derived.

Oberyn Martell's use of poison is viewed by many Westerosi nobles as proof of his moral laxity – as if his bisexuality and his bastards weren't enough. But, as Oberyn is quick to point out, morality in Dorne is different from that of the rest of Westeros: more modern, more liberal and, we might suggest, closer to that of George R.R. Martin himself. In Dorne, bastards aren't a source of shame, but pride; in Dorne, lust is not a sin, but something to be celebrated. They don't even observe male succession, allowing the oldest child of either gender to ascend the throne – a tradition that leads Dornish rebels to try to claim Princess Myrcella as the rightful Queen of Westeros, rather than her brother, Tommen.

And this question of morality lies at the core of *A Song of Ice and Fire* – indeed, the entire epic is at heart an examination of human ethics, of right and wrong. 'I've always taken it as a code,' Martin told *Time* magazine, 'William Faulkner's Nobel Prize acceptance speech from the early '50s, where he said that the human heart in conflict with itself was the only thing worth writing about. And I think that's true … I think the battle between good and evil is fought largely within the individual human heart, by the decisions that we make.'[14]

The moral struggles inherent in making crucial, life-or-death decisions is an issue that comes up again and again throughout *A Song of Ice and Fire*, and the answers are never simple. Seemingly benevolent deeds can have dire consequences – for example, Daenerys's decision to spare the life of the Godswife Mirri Maz Duur leads to the death of Khal Drogo and the collapse of his army – while even apparently monstrous acts, like the massacre at the Red Wedding, can have positive outcomes, at least for some: as Lord Tywin demands of his son Tyrion, 'explain to me why it is more noble to kill ten thousand men in battle than a dozen at dinner'.[15]

But it is another of Tywin Lannister's children who most exemplifies Martin's examination of morality. On the surface,

This twelfth-century illustration of an apothecary's shop shows shelves stocked with jars of herbs and medicines

Umbelliferae.

Conium maculatum L.

# 'A GOOD ACT DOES NOT WASH OUT THE BAD, NOR A BAD ACT THE GOOD'

Stannis Baratheon, *A Clash of Kings*[16]

Jaime Lannister is a paragon of beauty and virtue, 'tall and golden, with flashing green eyes and a smile that cut like a knife ... *this is what a king should look like*',[17] according to Jon Snow. But Jaime is also an unrepentant killer, a murderer of kings, whose first notable act in the story is to throw nine-year-old Bran Stark from a high window when he catches Jaime having sex with his own sister.

And yet, as the story unfolds, Jaime's character trajectory becomes one of redemption. Shamed in battle by Robb Stark, he is set free by Lady Catelyn and sent back to King's Landing under the watchful eye of Brienne of Tarth. When his sword hand is removed by the slobbering monster, Vargo Hoat, Jaime's entire personality begins to change. His bond with Brienne deepens, their relationship goes from loathing to grudging respect and, finally, trust, as Jaime gifts her his own Valyrian steel sword and sends her out to find Catelyn's missing daughters.

But how can someone who attempted to murder a child ever be redeemed? For Martin, it's all about context. 'Jaime isn't just trying to kill Bran because he's an annoying little kid,' the author explains. 'Bran has seen something that is basically a death sentence for Jaime, for Cersei, and their children ... Probably more people than not would ... kill someone else's child to save [their] own, even if that other child was innocent. These are the difficult decisions people make, and they're worth examining.'[18]

For Martin, the only truly irredeemable characters are those who never question themselves or their actions – those who, as Jojen Reed warns, 'hurt others just because they can'.[19] These are men like Gregor Clegane, the Mountain That Rides, who rapes and slaughters Elia Martell simply because his master Lord Tywin didn't tell him not to; or Ramsay Snow, the bastard of Bolton, who locks his wife in a tower until she eats her own fingers, before proceeding to hunt, flay, rape and butcher his way across the North. Beside these brutes, even murderers like Jaime Lannister, his brother Tyrion and Joffrey's 'pet dog' the Hound seem like paragons of virtue.

Part Four

# ESSOS

Chapter Ten

# THE FREE CITIES

In the Middle Ages, most of Europe was controlled by feudal monarchies held in place by ancient tradition, holy terror and aristocratic privilege. In Italy, however, something rather different happened. Following the collapse of the western Roman Empire, while the peninsula was still nominally under the control of various kingdoms, duchies and foreign powers, a new kind of nation began to emerge: the free state. Over the next millennium, these wealthy republics would transform not just Italy but the entire world, expanding into mighty maritime trading powers and sowing the seeds of modern capitalism. They would also engage in near-constant struggles for dominance, employing mercenary armies or 'free companies' to maintain their independence.

At the western extreme of the continent of Essos, the political landscape looks very similar. Following the destruction of Old Valyria in an apocalyptic firestorm, that nation's great empire fragmented into nine separate city-states: the island nations of Lorath, Lys, Tyrosh and Braavos, the trading ports of Myr, Pentos and Volantis; and the inland cities of Norvos and Qohor. And while alliances between these cities are not unknown – the pact known as the Triarchy between Myr, Lys and Tyrosh

would last for several decades, as depicted in *House of the Dragon* – they are just as likely to be found at one another's throats, jostling for power or fighting over disputed land.

In medieval Italy, perhaps the most powerful and certainly the best known of the free states was the Republic of Venice, a 'thalassocracy' or maritime republic founded on trade and later banking, with its own traditions and even its own language, Venetian, which is still spoken by many in the area today. Although centred on the ancient lagoon city and its surrounding regions, the Venetian Republic held territory in several countries, including Croatia, Slovenia, Greece and Cyprus, and operated a powerful navy alongside its fleets of trading vessels. Founded in the eighth century, the Republic would endure until 1797, when it would be torn apart during the war between Napoleon's French army and the Austrian Hapsburgs.

The similarity between Venice and one of the Free Cities in *A Song of Ice and Fire* is not a subtle one. Like Venice, Braavos is a lagoon city, 'a great sprawl of domes and towers and bridges, grey and gold and red. The hundred isles of Braavos in the sea.'[1] Like Venice, its canals are crowded with ships, big and small, and spanned by countless colourfully decorated bridges.

The entrance to the Venetian lagoon may not be straddled by a 120-m- (400-ft-) high bronze-and-granite statue – the Titan of Braavos, clearly inspired by the ancient Colossus of Rhodes – but both cities are dominated by a vast fortified arsenal that both defends the city and is used as a factory for the construction of ships and weaponry.

Braavos is, in fact, the only one of the Free Cities never to have been part of the Valyrian Empire: as the mysterious figure known only as the 'Kindly Man' tells Arya, 'We are a mongrel folk, the sons of slaves and whores and thieves. Our forebears came from half a hundred lands to this place of refuge, to escape the dragonlords who had enslaved them'.[2] And while the precise origins of Venice have been lost to time, it seems that the lagoon's original population were also refugees, escaping invasion by Germanic tribes to the north. For many years ruled by the Byzantine or eastern Roman Empire, in AD 726 Venice revolted and installed its own duke or *doge*, a title that would endure through the time of the Republic. In Braavos, the city's ruler is known as the Sealord, who, like the *doge*, is elected by a council of the city's most notable people and serves for life.

But there's one further tradition that ties Braavos and Venice even more closely together: finance. In Braavos,

'WESTEROSI MAY
BE WARRIORS, BUT WE
BRAAVOSI ARE TRADERS.
LET US TRADE.'

The Sealord of Braavos, *Fire and Blood*[5]

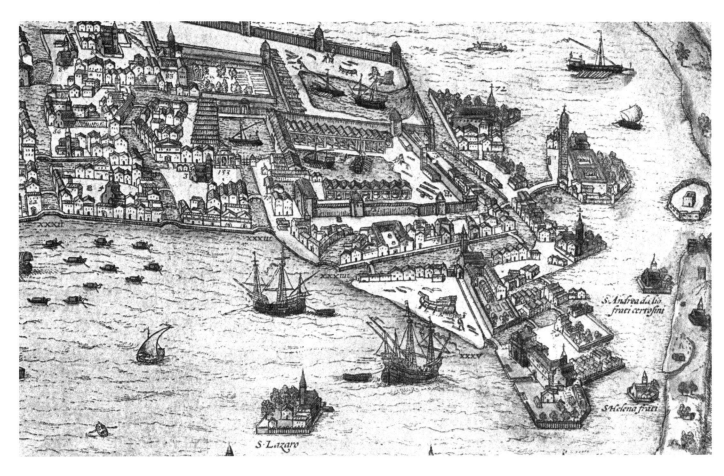

**OPPOSITE**
Mighty colossus:
the Titan of Braavos
stands sentinel over
the passage into this
bustling port city

**TOP**
The arsenal of Venice,
from the sixteenth-
century map book
*Civitates Orbis Terrarum*
by Georg Braun and
Frans Hogenberg

**BOTTOM**
Ancient Venice as
depicted in *Miracle
of the Relic of the Holy
Cross at the Bridge of
San Lorenzo* (1500),
by Gentile Bellini

# 'THE IRON BANK WILL HAVE ITS DUE, THEY SAY'

Grand Maester Pycelle, *A Feast for Crows*[4]

the Iron Bank has risen to become the most powerful economic entity in the known world, a place to which 'kings, princes, archons, triarchs, and merchants beyond count travel from the ends of the earth to seek loans'.[5] In Westeros, the crown owes millions to this foreign institution – and while the Lannisters may be famed for always paying their debts, the Iron Bank are known for always collecting theirs. As Jon Snow reflects, 'when princes failed to repay the Iron Bank, new princes sprung up from nowhere and took their thrones'.[6] Not coincidentally, Braavos has become the wealthiest of the Free Cities – Volantis may be larger and more powerful, but Braavos is where the money is.

Similarly, Venice's great wealth was founded largely on banking – indeed, the city was the site of the world's first merchant bank. For centuries, the practice of lending with interest, or 'usury', had been outlawed by the Catholic Church. Jewish moneylenders could provide credit and insurance services, but they were not allowed to own property outside of the established Jewish ghetto, so like the 'Thin Man' that Arya is sent to murder in HBO's *Game of Thrones,* they would operate from a bench or *banco* in the piazza, from which we derive the word 'bank'.

But when a convenient (if complicated) loophole was finally found to circumvent the Catholic law against usury, everything changed. The newly established Bank of Venice would soon become the most powerful financial institution in the world, though it would not be the only one – other Italian banks soon followed, lending money across Europe and financing, among many other conflicts, the English pacification of Scotland and the Hundred Years War. But the Bank of Venice would remain the most notable: as Professor Larrington writes, 'It's no coincidence that Shakespeare's exploration of the theme of international finance is called *The Merchant of Venice*, for its plot reflects exactly the meshing together of finance ... that made the city so rich and powerful'.[7]

According to *The World of Ice and Fire*, the roots of the Iron Bank stretch back 'to the beginnings of the city',[8] when a handful of the refugees who first settled the lagoon secreted their valuables in an old iron mine for safe keeping. As the city grew, these treasures increased and, ultimately, these first founders – 16 men and 7 women – began to make loans, first to their fellow Braavosi, then further afield. By the time of the War of Five Kings the Iron Bank is a global enterprise, whose 'envoys cross

# 'There are old sellswords and bold sellswords, but no old bold sellswords'

Brown Ben Plumm, *A Storm of Swords*[9]

the world, oft upon the bank's own ships, and merchants, lords and even kings treat with them almost as equals'.[10]

Not surprisingly, such wealth has attracted the jealousy of rival cities, and over the centuries Braavos has fought no fewer than six wars against her immediate neighbour, Pentos, over land and the rights of slaves (a practice that Braavos – given its history – detests, and that Pentos has now outlawed). In four of these conflicts, thanks to its mighty navy, its heavily fortified city and its long tradition of sword fighting – as exemplified by the city's famous 'water dancers' – Braavos emerged victorious.

But while Venice may have had a powerful navy, the same could not be said of its land forces. With only a small native population, the city was not large enough to raise the kind of army it needed to defend itself and to claim further territory – but it did have the money to buy one. And so, like many of its fellow free states, Venice recruited mercenaries: warriors both foreign and domestic, often the veterans of multiple campaigns, brought together under the name 'free companies'.

Perhaps the most storied of these – thanks in large part to one of George R.R. Martin's favourite authors – was the so-called White Company, initially known as the Great Company of English and Germans, and later as the English Company. Founded by a German nobleman named Albert Sterz, who had fought on the English side in the (then ongoing) Hundred Years War, the company was made up of soldiers from France, Italy, Germany, Hungary and the

British Isles, among them the English minor nobleman, John Hawkwood. Arriving in Italy in 1361, the company would fight for several Italian cities, including Pisa and Milan, and for the pope himself. Following Sterz's departure in 1363, Hawkwood assumed command and would become famous across Europe. Upon his death at the ripe old age of 60 he would be memorialized with a portrait on the wall of the Duomo in Florence, painted by Paolo Uccello at the behest of the Medici family, and accompanied by a Latin inscription that translates as 'John Hawkwood, British knight, most prudent leader of his age and most expert in the art of war'.

Hawkwood's adventures would also inspire one of the formative works of historical fiction. Published in 1891, *The White Company* was written by Sir Arthur Conan Doyle at a time when he was desperate to be known for something other than his most famous creation, Sherlock Holmes. Writing to his mother the same year to complain of his success, Conan Doyle admitted that 'I think of slaying Holmes ... and winding him up for good and all' (she wrote back pleading, 'You won't! You can't! You mustn't!'[11] – though of course, eventually, he did). Though playing fast and loose with the facts – *The White Company* is set largely in Britain and France, rather than in Italy, and populated mostly by fictional characters – this lively adventure story would become hugely popular with schoolboys across Britain and America. It would also find favour with George R.R. Martin, who chose it as one of his

Free rider: the monument to Sir John Hawkwood, painted by Paolo Uccello (1436) in the Florence Cathedral

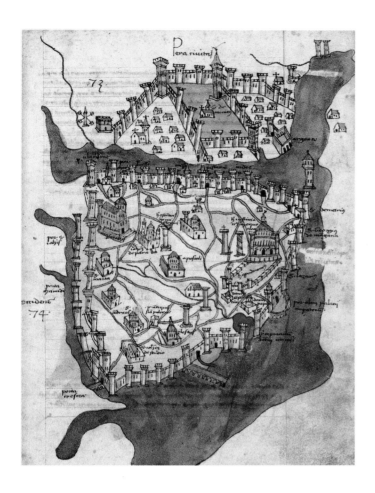

Reading Recommendations, writing that 'there's still great stuff to be found in … Sir Arthur Conan Doyle's *The White Company* (he wrote more than just Sherlock Holmes)'[12] – a sentiment that would surely have gratified the author, had he lived to read it.

And Martin evidently found more in the book than just a ripping yarn, because the similarity between the free companies of medieval Europe and those found in *A Song of Ice and Fire* is inescapable. Forged, for the most part, in the 'century of blood' that followed the Doom of Valyria, these mercenary bands range from the disreputable and bloodthirsty likes of the Brave Companions – known as the Bloody Mummers, and hired by Tywin Lannister to pillage the Riverlands – to well-organized and respected organizations like the Golden Company. Formed by a bastard son of King Aegon IV Targaryen and populated largely by the sons of his fellow Westerosi exiles, the Golden Company was, until recently, captained by a man named Ser Myles

Toyne, a 'soldier to the bone … fierce but always fair,'[13] who bears more than a little similarity to his historical counterpart John Hawkwood.

When we first encounter the Golden Company in *A Dance With Dragons*, they have ended their contract with the free city of Myr and are on their way to the sprawling metropolis of Volantis, hoping to join forces with Daenerys Targaryen. Like Braavos, Volantis is a city with a proud history and a globe-spanning reputation: after the fall of Valyria, it was the Volantenes who attempted to claim their place as the successors to that mighty empire, just as when the Roman Empire collapsed it was the city of Constantinople that strove to seize Rome's crown.

Like Constantinople – or Byzantium, as it was known to the ancients – Volantis lies on a river believed to mark the border between west and east. Both rivers are spanned by a great bridge – for Volantis, the Long Bridge; in ancient Constantinople (and modern-day Istanbul), the Bosphorus Bridge, versions of which have been constructed as far back as 500 BC.

But, as always with Martin, nothing is straightforward. With its cloying humidity and political factions named Tigers and Elephants, Volantis feels closer in mood and climate to the great cities of ancient India than to Europe or even the Middle East. Indeed, the name given to the city's distinctive elephant-drawn carts, *hathay*, clearly echoes the Hindu word for elephant, *hathi* (also the name of the elephant leader in Rudyard Kipling's *The Jungle Book*, 1894), while the city's great river, the Mother Rhoyne, might take inspiration from the *Ganga Mata*, the Mother Ganges, greatest of all Indian rivers.

The Volantenes also share one key export with ancient India: not a spice or a jewel, but a game. '*Cyvasse*, the game was called,' Ser Arys Oakheart explains in *A Feast for Crows*. 'It had come … on a trading galley from Volantis.'[14] Though Ser Arys personally finds the game 'maddening', he attempts to describe it for the reader: 'There were ten different pieces, each with its own attributes and powers, and the board would change from game to game, depending on how the players arrayed their home squares.'[15]

Among these pieces are light horse, heavy horse, a trebuchet, a dragon, an elephant and a king whose assassination is the aim of the game. Otherwise, even George R.R. Martin admits that he doesn't fully understand the rules: 'I've actually turned down a number of offers from game companies who want to market *cyvasse*, and come up with rules,' he told an audience in 2015. 'But you know, some things are better suggested than shown ... It's a game of great complexity, it's a game of great profundity, it's a game like chess, which is half a thousand years old. Is it likely that any game company ... could come up with a game to equal chess? No!'[16]

Though the rules of chess as we understand them were codified in fifteenth-century Europe, the roots of the game go back much further: archaeologists in the Indus Valley have unearthed boards resembling those used in chess from as far back as 2,000 BC, while the modern game owes many of its rules to the sixth-century Indian game of *chaturanga*. Played on a board of 8x8 squares known as *ashtāpada*, the game included familiar pieces like the king, the knight (known as *ashva* or horse) and rook (known as *ratha*, or chariot), alongside since-replaced tokens such as the *mantri*, or minister, the forerunner of the queen, and the *gaja*, or elephant, who would become the bishop.

George R.R. Martin's own history with chess goes back to childhood, and for many years the game would be more than just a pastime for him, but a professional calling. 'Chess was a huge part of my life in high school, in college, and especially in the years after college,' he wrote on his 'Not a Blog'. 'I was the captain of my high school chess team, the founder and president of my college chess club ... The first two great loves of my life were girls I met at the chess club.'[17] In his 20s, Martin even managed to make a living from the game. Having largely stopped playing after achieving the rank of Expert – 'I chose writing instead'[18] – he would continue to supplement his income by directing chess

tournaments, travelling from city to city to oversee competition matches. He even wrote an article for *Analog* magazine entitled 'The Computer Was a Fish', about the rise of computer chess.[19]

So, although it may be 'many, many decades since I last ran a chess tournament or even played a game of chess',[20] it's perhaps unsurprising that the game would eventually emerge in Martin's fiction – and not just in the form of *cyvasse*. The scenes of warfare in *A Song of Ice and Fire* must also owe more than a little to his history as a chess player – though they may be bloodier and more hectic than those fought upon the chequered board, the battles in Martin's writing nonetheless illustrate the vital importance of strategic thinking, and the essentially game-like nature of warfare. It's right there in the title of the first book, after all.

**ABOVE**
The August 1972 issue of *Analog* magazine featuring GRRM's article about computer chess

**OPPOSITE**
Painted in the nineteenth century by an anonymous artist, *The Chaturanga Party* shows two Indian women engaged in the game that would become chess

## Chapter Eleven

# VAES DOTHRAK

The first of the Free Cities that we visit in *A Song of Ice and Fire* is Pentos, a maze of square towers and tiled roofs with a distinctly Mediterranean flavour. It's here that young Daenerys Targaryen is betrothed and wed to the Dothraki horselord Khal Drogo, but the newlyweds don't remain in Pentos long. Following the wedding, Drogo and his khalasar set out across the great grass steppes of the Dothraki Sea, bound for the city of Vaes Dothrak.

These vast empty plains were once part of the Kingdom of Sarnor, a powerful civilization that lasted for two millennia. But following the Doom of Valyria, the Dothraki came from the east, pillaging their way across this ancient kingdom. United for the first time under the legendary Khal Mengo, the nomadic horselords sacked and burned the towns and cities of Sarnor, butchering the people of the steppes and taking their wealth for themselves. Since then, the Dothraki have themselves fragmented, breaking up into countless roaming khalasars, waging war on each other and on anyone foolish enough to stand up to them. By far the largest of these khalasars is the one headed by Khal Drogo, son of Khal Barbo, a warrior undefeated in battle, and the ruler of some 40,000 followers.

According to George R.R. Martin, the Dothraki were 'fashioned as an amalgam of a number of steppe and plains cultures ... Mongols and Huns, certainly, but also Alans, Sioux, Cheyenne, and various other Amerindian tribes ... seasoned with a dash of pure fantasy'.[1] It's the first of these whose influence is undoubtedly the strongest: the Mongols, whose horse-mounted warriors swept across Asia in the twelfth century, and particularly the followers of Temüjin, conqueror of the largest land empire in history. Martin doesn't even try to hide it: while Drogo and the other leaders of the Dothraki take on the noble title of Khal, the honorific employed by their real-life inspiration was only one letter removed: Genghis Khan.

Working from multiple sources of varying reliability, historians have struggled to build a precise picture of Temüjin's early life, even down to the year of his birth, which might have been anywhere from 1155 to 1167. But most agree that Temüjin was, like Drogo, the son of a chieftain: Yesügei, leader of the Borjigin clan of Inner Mongolia. Born, according to legend, clutching a clot of blood – the sure sign of a natural warrior – Temüjin was betrothed at age eight to the daughter of a neighbouring chieftain. But when his father Yesügei died, the Borjigin clan were

scattered, and young Temüjin was reduced to living off the land, eating roots, nuts and whatever he could hunt.

Following his marriage at 15 to the girl Yesügei had chosen, Temüjin's fortunes began to improve. Allying himself with his father's friend, Toghrul Khan of the Kerait tribe, Temüjin declared war against the most powerful Mongol warrior on the steppes, Wang Khan, whom he defeated. Though many saw him as an upstart – among them his own uncles – Temüjin's power grew, and by 1206 he had defeated every one of his rivals and was crowned Emperor of the Mongol State. Taking the title of Genghis Khan – though the name is hard to transliterate, and might variously be spelled *Chingis*, *Jinghis* or *Jengiz* – Temüjin united the tribes, reorganized his army and set his sights on conquest.

The details of Genghis Khan's extraordinary takeover of Central Asia are far too elaborate to go into here, but suffice it to say that by the time of his death in 1227, Temüjin ruled over a land empire twice the size of that conquered by the Romans, and he'd done it all in just two decades. From the Caspian Sea on the borders of Europe to the Sea of Japan far to the east, armies had been routed, cities sacked and their people brought into the vast Mongolian Empire, usually by force. In the wake of

# 'THE DOTHRAKI FOLLOW ONLY THE STRONG'

Ser Jorah Mormont, *A Game of Thrones*[2]

The conqueror:
a portrait of Temüjin,
known as Genghis
Khan, by an unknown
fourteenth-century artist

# 'The Dothraki sacked cities and plundered kingdoms, they did not rule them'

Thoughts of Daenerys Targaryen, *A Clash of Kings*[3]

**TOP**
This fourteenth-century artwork depicts the conquest of Baghdad by the Mongols under Genghis Khan in the year 1258

**BOTTOM**
Home of the horse lords: the tent city of Vaes Dothrak, from season 6 of *Game of Thrones*

his death the empire would expand even further: led by Temüjin's sons, the Mongol armies would invade India and Korea, lay siege to cities as far afield as Kiev and Baghdad, and kill, enslave or displace countless millions of people. The tales of Mongol aggression against foreign cities are horrifying: employing a strategy of total warfare, Genghis Khan's armies wouldn't just kill rival soldiers, they'd annihilate entire populations, leading many historians to claim Temüjin as the first to practise a policy of genocide.

Yet others see him very differently. In modern-day Mongolia, Genghis Khan is lauded as a hero – a symbol of national identity, particularly among the young. And indeed, the Mongol Empire was not merely one of brutal repression. Given its size, the empire was necessarily one of the most ethnically diverse ever recorded, with positions of power reported to have been granted on the basis of a man's merits, not his ethnic or religious background. As historian George Lane writes: 'Genghis Khan was selective in his destruction ... Craftsmen and artisans, poets and painters, and clerics and holy men of all faiths were spared the fate of their countrymen.'[4]

Under a legal code known as Yassa, Genghis Khan laid down rules ensuring the toleration of all religious beliefs,

bluntly stating that 'all religions were to be respected and that no preference was to be shown to any of them'. The Yassa also offered rules for the fair pillaging of cities – 'It is forbidden, under the death penalty, to pillage the enemy before the general commanding gives permission, but after that permission is given, the soldier must have the same opportunity as the officer.' As well as the treatment of non-combatants – 'minors not higher than a cartwheel may not be killed in war ... also, abduction of women and sexual assault and/or abuse of women is punishable by death' – though these seem to have been followed only when the conquerors felt it appropriate. Elsewhere, the Yassa also offers rules concerning everything from bastardy, adultery and sodomy ('punishable by death', inevitably) to the cleanliness and comportment of the imperial population: it was 'forbidden to bathe or wash garments in running water during thunder', and also 'forbidden to wash clothing until completely worn out'.[5] Evidently, the army of Genghis Khan had standards to maintain.

Dothraki culture, too, fuses brutality with honour, and strict tradition with moral flexibility. Like the Mongols, they practise religious toleration: while the Dothraki do have a religion of their own, worshipping a horse god – obviously – alongside the feminine moon and masculine sun, they do not persecute others for their beliefs. They will, however, happily ransack temples for their gold and statues, which they carry back to Vaes Dothrak, deep in the heart of the Dothraki Sea.

Though referred to as a city, Vaes Dothrak is closer to a giant encampment, 'a vastness without walls or limits, its broad windswept streets paved in grass and mud and carpeted with wildflowers',[6] whose only permanent residents are the *dosh khaleen*, the ancient wise women whose laws and prophecies are followed even by the most powerful khals. For the Dothraki are still a nomadic people, who 'consider the earth to be their mother, and think it sinful to cut her flesh with plows [sic] and spades and axes'[7] – hence their genocidal rewilding of the grasslands.

# 'In this place ... all Dothraki were one blood, one khalasar, one herd'

Thoughts of Daenerys Targaryen, *A Game of Thrones*[8]

The Mongols, too, originated as nomads, but they didn't all stay that way. In 1218, Genghis Khan gathered his armies at Karakorum in the heart of the steppes, and this location would ultimately become the capital of the Mongol Empire. Though building did not begin in earnest until 1235 – before which the site was a yurt town, not unlike Vaes Dothrak – Karakorum would eventually become a true walled city, with a domed temple and a palace for the khan containing a great tree fashioned from silver and coiled by a golden serpent. Small by European standards, the city would not last long as the Mongol capital: in 1260, Kublai Khan abandoned it in favour of his own city of Shangdu, or Xanadu.

Karakorum would, however, remain a key stop along the southernmost course of the Silk Road, the historical land route from Europe, Africa and the Middle East to China and the Far East from the second until the fifteenth centuries. While for much of its existence, travel along the Silk Road was treacherous due to predatory bandits and natural impediments, under the rein of Kublai Khan merchants were protected as they travelled through the Mongol Empire. He even went a step further and 'made foreign traders exempt from taxation', giving them 'privileges not enjoyed by his subjects'.[9] The Dothraki,

too, offer protection to those merchants willing to brave the overland journey from the Free Cities to the lands of the east. As a result, Vaes Dothrak has become a bustling mercantile hub, 'where the caravans from Yi Ti and Asshai and the Shadow Lands came to trade'.[10]

Another aspect of Dothraki culture that resembles that of the Mongols is their fierce dedication to brotherhood. 'Every Khal had his bloodriders,' Daenerys observes in *A Game of Thrones*. '"Blood of my blood", Drogo called them, and so it was: they shared a single life.'[11] In Mongolian culture, a friendship bound in blood was equally sacred. Temüjin's first great ally, Toghrul, had been a blood brother to his father, Yesügei, while Temüjin's own blood brother, Jamukha, was one of his oldest friends, assisting Temüjin in reclaiming his wife, Borte, when she was abducted by a rival tribe. However, this particular bond of blood would not endure: in 1201, those tribes not yet allied to Temüjin banded together and chose Jamukha to lead them, creating a rift that would end in Jamukha's execution.

But as Martin admits, the Mongols weren't the only inspiration behind the Dothraki. Indeed, blood brotherhood was also vital to another culture who roamed the Eurasian steppes north of

**TOP**
Wagons west: this detail from the 1380 *Catalan Atlas* depicts caravans travelling on the great Silk Road

**BOTTOM**
An aerial view of the modern-day Kharkhorin Erdene Zuu Monastery on the site of what was once Karakorum in Mongolia

the Black Sea centuries before the rise of the Mongol Empire, from around the ninth until the third century BC: the Scythians. The precise parameters of that name may be disputed – 'Scythian' has traditionally been a loose description covering multiple peoples including the Cimmerians, Massagetae and Sarmatians – but their similarity to the Dothraki is clear. Both are horse-mounted nomads who sleep in tents or yurts; both wear clothes made from leather, felt and fur; and both wear medallions fashioned from bronze and gold – indeed, the artworks left behind by the Scythians are among the most ornate and beautiful relics of the ancient world. And while historians may be divided on whether the Scythians themselves worshipped horses, many of their fellow Eurasian tribes certainly did.

Like the Dothraki, the Scythians were also trained from an early age in the use of bows, spears and swords. Supposedly the inventors of the saddle, they were among the earliest and most deadly proponents of horse-mounted warfare. At its height, the Scythian Empire stretched from the Caucasus Mountains to the northern parts of Syria, and their nomadic armies fought battles with legendary commanders including Darius the Great of Persia and Philip II of Macedonia, father of Alexander the Great.

This technique of fighting on horseback also ties the Dothraki to another of Martin's stated influences: the 'Sioux, Cheyenne, and various other Amerindian tribes'.[12] Other links between the Dothraki and Native Americans include the use of oil in their hair – in *A Game of Thrones*, the Dothraki are seen to have 'greased their long braids with fat from the rendering pits',[13] while Native Americans were known to use bear's fat to make their hair shine – and their habit of raiding neighbouring tribes and making off with goods, animals and even people.

However, as historian and blogger, Bret Devereaux, points out, the purpose of such raids was very different for the Native Americans than it seems to be for the nomads of Essos. For the Dothraki, human prisoners – like those 'Lamb Men' corralled by Drogo's khalasar on his way west – are to be sold as slaves, viewed as lesser beings only fit for death and servitude. For the American plains' tribes, however, 'the capture of women and children to enhance tribal strength in the long term was a core objective in raiding'[14] – indeed, it may have been necessary to maintain tribal numbers, given that some would inevitably be killed in battle.

Instead, Devereaux argues that Martin's 'primary inspiration ... seems to come from deeply flawed Hollywood

**ABOVE**
Equine art: a Scythian comb (left) and necklace (middle) from around the fourth century BC; and an Etruscan statue of a Scythian warrior on horseback (right) from the same period

**OPPOSITE**
Lights, camera, charge! Cast and crew on the Monument Valley set of 1939's *Stagecoach*

depictions of nomadic peoples ...
The Dothraki are not an amalgam of
the Sioux or the Mongols, but rather an
amalgam of *Stagecoach* (1939) and *The
Conqueror* (1956)'.[15] These are the titles
of two films starring John Wayne, the
first a classic western directed by John
Ford and culminating in an attack by
mounted Apache warriors, the second a
deeply dubious biopic of Genghis Khan
which is routinely listed among the
worst films ever made, and not just for
Wayne's slanted eye make-up and Fu
Manchu moustache. Both would almost
certainly have screened on TV during
George R.R. Martin's childhood, along
with many other Hollywood westerns and
TV serials like *Wagon Train* (1957–65) and
*The Lone Ranger* (1949–57), many of them
offering questionable portrayals of Native
American peoples – though whether any
of them did directly influence his creation
of the Dothraki remains unproven.

But there's no doubt that one of the
films Devereaux cites did have a direct
impact on HBO's *Game of Thrones*. In
season 7, as Jaime Lannister leads a wagon
train loaded with Tyrell grain through a
region of Westeros that looks suspiciously
like Arizona's Monument Valley – the
shooting location for countless westerns,
including *Stagecoach* – the sound of high-
pitched ululation is heard in the distance.

Moments later, the Lannister forces are
attacked by a horde of mounted Dothraki
screamers, thundering across the plains
and firing arrows from horseback in direct
homage to the climax of *Stagecoach*.
While thrilling in the moment, this
association between the attacking
Dothraki and the bloodthirsty Apache
warriors of Ford's film does feel rather
trite, and potentially offensive – a concern
that will become somewhat more pressing
as we draw towards the end of our tour.

**OPPOSITE**
Wild east: John Wayne
in dubious make-up
as Genghis Khan in
*The Conqueror* (1956)

**ABOVE**
Dothraki screamers
thunder into battle in
*Game of Thrones*

Chapter Twelve

# SLAVER'S BAY AND BEYOND

For the citizens of medieval Europe, the lands that lay to the east were both wondrous and terrible, at once a trackless wilderness filled with barbarous savages and a world of opportunity, adventure and unimaginable wealth. Very few would ever have paused to wonder if they might have anything in common with the people of these far-flung lands – they were heathens, monsters, closer to beasts than men. From the religious massacres of the Crusades to the brutal exploitation of the slave and spice trades, those in the West proved time and again their disdain for anyone who didn't look, think and worship like themselves.

Over the centuries, these ideas would become deeply embedded in Western thought, art and literature, creating what, in his 1978 book of the same name,[1] the Palestinian-American cultural critic Edward Said called 'orientalism': a prejudicial, Eurocentric viewpoint towards the people of the east, and particularly towards Arabic cultures. From heroic myths of Alexander the Great's conquests and the cruel treatment of Christian martyrs to popular modern epics like the film 300 (2006) – which presents the white-skinned Greeks as musclebound heroes while their Persian adversaries are grotesque monsters – this prejudice has persisted for hundreds of years and has only recently begun to be unpicked and questioned.

For the conscious reader, it's impossible to ignore the orientalist nature of A Song of Ice and Fire. With a handful of exceptions, the people of the east – whether that's the Dothraki, their rustic victims the Lamb Men or the inhabitants of Slaver's Bay – are depicted either as bloodthirsty brutes or as helpless victims, as oppressors or oppressed, with very little in between. And when the tables turn and the slaves become the masters, these liberated prisoners behave exactly as their erstwhile persecutors did, becoming killers and even slavers themselves.

Among the key aspects of orientalism is that it maintains a Western perspective at all times: whether Eastern peoples and cultures are depicted sympathetically or otherwise, we're never given a chance to see the world through their eyes. And, so far in A Song of Ice and Fire, that's largely been the case: even in A Feast for Crows and A Dance With Dragons, with their great spread of point-of-view characters, the only Essos-born figures we hear from are the Norvoshi guard captain Areo Hotah and – for one solitary chapter – the Asshai-born Red Priestess, Melisandre.

Even the pale-skinned Qartheen, the citizens of that great city of merchants and princes, remain aloof, inscrutable and untrustworthy, eager to exploit Daenerys and her dragons. For Professor Larrington, that's hardly surprising: 'the fact that there's no native character whose viewpoint we share, no insider who can mediate the Qartheen to us, makes understanding this eastern city of wonder impossible.'[2]

Of course, there are mitigating factors at work. It could certainly be argued that the people of Westeros are no great improvement over their eastern counterparts, and are just as willing to murder, exploit and pillage. The fact that almost every point-of-view character in the books hails from that continent might also suggest that Martin is playing on medieval myths of the 'barbaric' east, offering a fantastical vision more akin to the way medieval people would've imagined the east, rather than anything approaching reality. Still, as the story unfolds in further books, perhaps we might be allowed to view the world through eastern eyes – to see, for example, how the young scribe, Missandei of Naath, views her beloved Queen Daenerys, or get a glimpse into the hopes and ambitions of the noble Unsullied guard captain, Grey Worm.

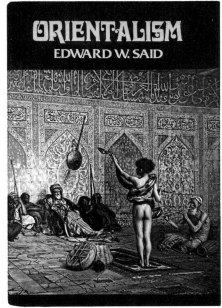

**TOP**
Author and academic
Edward Said alongside
a first edition of his
best-known work,
1978's *Orientalism*

**BOTTOM**
White saviour?
Daenerys Targaryen
(Emilia Clarke, centre)
with her advisors
(left to right): Missandei
(Nathalie Emmanuel),
Tyrion (Peter Dinklage),
Varys (Conleth Hill)
and Grey Worm
(Jacob Anderson)

Des obriſten kamerling
Vnd Trüchſes

# 'The Unsullied have something better than strength. They have discipline.'

Kraznys Mo Nakloz, *A Storm of Swords*[3]

The Unsullied are, of course, those slave soldiers who have been kidnapped and castrated as children, brutally trained in the arts of war by the Wise Masters of Astapor and sold across Essos as the most fearsome fighting force known to man. According to George R.R. Martin, their inspirations included medieval armies like the mamluks – slave soldiers who fought as mercenaries across the medieval world, but particularly in Egypt – and the Janissary corps of the Ottoman Empire, whose prowess at battles like the capture of Constantinople in 1453 and the Siege of Rhodes in 1522 would pass into legend. Made up of boys and young men kidnapped from their families and transported to Turkey, the Janissary corps would be housed together in barracks and drilled relentlessly until they became, like the Unsullied, the most feared fighting force of their age. Often taken from Christian countries – there was a law against the enslavement of fellow Muslims – these children would be forcibly converted to Islam and encouraged to view the sultan not just as their master but as an almost godlike father figure.

But the differences between Martin's Unsullied and real-world slave soldiers are just as notable. Janissary troops, for instance, would be paid a regular wage throughout their time of service,

and after the age of 40 they could leave the corps to marry and engage in business, ultimately becoming a wealthy and respected caste within Ottoman society. They may have risked their lives for the sultan, but in return they were treated far better than regular soldiers, with their own camps, their own cooks and even travelling musicians.

And although many Janissaries would have been forcibly circumcised as part of their conversion to Islam, they would most definitely not have been castrated. Indeed, in the real world, castration would be one of the least effective things one could do to a prospective soldier, given that it reduces the production of testosterone, thereby limiting aggressive behaviour. Rather, eunuchs in medieval times tended to take on more courtly roles, as advisors and bureaucrats, singers and entertainers, and, of course, as masters of the harem – indeed, the word *eunuch* translates from the Greek as 'bed guardian'.

Though they had been a feature at court since the time of the Persian and early Roman Empires, it was in the Byzantine Empire that the employment of eunuchs was most commonplace. As historian Kathryn Ringrose writes: 'accepted for centuries as a functionally legitimate group, eunuchs were a feature of Byzantine society throughout its history ... from the founding of Constantinople in 324 to its capture by the Turks in 1453.'[4] Able, like the Red Keep's own 'master of whisperers' Lord Varys, to wield great influence within the court, these eunuchs were often employed as mediators, 'viewed as the best people to navigate certain spaces: between the sacred and profane, the political and the social'.[5] Eunuchs were even able to define their own gender roles, with 'some ... identified as male, while others identified (or were read) as belonging to a gender spectrum'.[6]

And some eunuchs did take on military roles. As well as being the imperial treasurer, the sixth-century Byzantine eunuch, Narses, was also a respected and apparently fearless general: when the Empress Sofia attempted to chastise Narses by telling him that 'he ought to be weaving with the ladies, Narses replied, "I will weave such a web around you that

Top hats: an illustration of Janissary soldiers from the sixteenth-century work *Pictures from Turkish Folk Life* by Heinrich Hendrowski

you'll not be able to break through it as long as you live"'.[8] Meanwhile, according to Professor Jonathan Hsy, in Tang-era China 'eunuchs played a significant role in court life and bureaucracy, with the Chief Eunuch being in charge of the military'.[9] Some centuries later, during the Ming dynasty, a eunuch named Zheng He even rose to become an admiral in the Chinese navy, commanding what was then the largest armada in the world.

Whether such powerful eunuchs might be found in the lands that lie even further east remains to be discovered. Beyond Slaver's Bay, we find cities such as New Ghis – once part of the Ghiscari Empire that ruled this part of the world before the rise of Valyria – and, of course, Qarth, an ancient metropolis that claims itself as the birthplace of civilization. Close to Qarth lie the Jade Gates, which link the Summer Sea – home to the tropical realms of Naath and the Basilisk Isles – to the far more mysterious Jade Sea, and which are presumably inspired by the aforementioned Pillars of Hercules (see page 110) situated at the mouth of the Mediterranean.

Beyond Qarth, our knowledge of the world is based largely on rumour and hearsay: tales of the Golden Empire of Yi Ti, which clearly owes much to historical China, and the island of Leng, whose people are said to grow up to 2.4 m (8 ft) tall. Finally, there's Asshai-by-the-Shadow, a port city on the far shore of the Jade Sea 'that has stood here since the world began and will stand here until it ends'.[10] Beyond the walls of Asshai lie the Shadow Lands, where nothing grows except ghost grass, and no one treads except the sorcerous Shadowbinders.

Again, in these sailors' tales of far-flung lands and rumoured monstrosities, we hear the echo of medieval myths, of half-understood reports of strange people and peculiar beasts whose pelts would be returned to Europe only to be inexpertly stuffed and displayed to a fascinated public. We think of Marco Polo, setting off along the Silk Road and returning with thrilling stories of mountain clans and distant empires, and of *Gulliver's Travels*, that 1726 satire on traveller's tales that

## 'The world is one great web, and a man dare not touch a single strand lest all the others tremble'

Magister Illyrio, *A Dance With Dragons*[7]

nonetheless managed to become as widely read as any real narrative.

And, of course, we think of maps: medieval charts drawn on parchment, ringed by fantastical sketches of whales and sea monsters, and peppered with blank spaces scribbled with the inscription 'here be dragons'. The nobles of Westeros set great store in maps. There's the Painted Table of Dragonstone, whose surface depicts 'the Seven Kingdoms as they had been in Aegon's day; rivers and mountains, castles and cities, lakes and forests'.[11] There's the ancient leather map of the Riverlands, unrolled by Robb Stark as he plans his war against Tywin Lannister. And there's the detailed map of the North, that Jon Snow consults in *A Dance With Dragons* to guide Stannis Baratheon towards the clans of the mountains – the Wulls, the Norreys and the Liddles.

Then there are the maps featured in the books themselves, initially sketched by George R.R. Martin before being refined and expanded for publication, first by James Sinclair and later by Jeffrey L. Ward. In 2012, these maps would be published as a boxed set of twelve detailed illustrations drawn by cartographer Jonathan Roberts of the Fantastic Maps blog, under the name *The Lands of Ice and Fire*. But whichever map they choose to consult,

The stunning *Catalan
Atlas*, completed in
1375 and attributed
to the cartographer
Abraham Cresques

# 'THE WORLD GROWS A LITTLE DARKER EVERY DAY'

Thoughts of Catelyn Stark, *A Storm of Swords*[12]

there's never a risk that readers of *A Song of Ice and Fire* will find themselves unable to navigate this invented world.

In the real Middle Ages, things weren't so straightforward. In fact, medieval Europeans were surprisingly inept at making maps, particularly when compared to their antecedents the Romans, or to their contemporaries in China and the Middle East. As cartographical historian P.D.A. Harvey writes: 'Maps were practically unknown ... Each was drawn for strictly limited purposes, with one class of user in mind – the Mediterranean navigator, the long-distance traveller by land, the law-court judging a dispute, the educated person seeking instruction in distant lands and customs. What it showed and how it showed it depended on what purpose it was to serve.'[13]

Of course, most medieval people didn't tend to travel very far from their homes, with the exception of pilgrimages, for which they preferred to consult written instructions rather than visual references: extensive travel guides detailing the routes to be taken by pilgrims were not uncommon and featured everything from warnings about quicksand to the best place to sit on the boat from Venice to Jaffa. The larger world maps that we think of when we imagine medieval maps – like the vast, gorgeously detailed *Mappa Mundi* drawn in 1300 and now housed in Hereford – tended to be symbolic rather than realistic, 'designed to help explain the theological position of man in the natural and supernatural world',[14] with the relative size of particular locations skewed by factors such as religious significance. Using one of these as a guide would result in the traveller getting very lost indeed.

There were exceptions, however. Drawn in 1375 and now housed in the *Bibliothèque nationale de France*, the *Catalan Atlas* was produced by the Majorcan Cartographical School, a predominantly Jewish map-making centre famed for its accuracy. Among the most important of all medieval maps, the atlas bears a remarkable fidelity to the real world, which it depicts with Jerusalem in the centre and includes references to the African empire of Mali, the Sultanate of Delhi, the Great Wall of China and the Golden Horde of the Mongols. As a result, it also displays a notable similarity, at least in outline, to the map of the Known World included in *The Lands of Ice and Fire* – here, at least, is a map we can imagine the sailors of Oldtown and Braavos using to navigate the trade routes to far-flung lands.

But while, as we've seen, *A Song of Ice and Fire* may take a great deal of influence from the medieval world, it does not – at least according to its author – bear significant similarity with the modern one. Like his forebear J.R.R. Tolkien, George R.R. Martin has no time for allegory, or for those who attempt to draw parallels between his work and contemporary events. 'The people who try to apply that are as wrong as the people who tried to do that with Tolkien, talking about *Lord of the Rings* being about World War II,' he said in 2017. 'It wasn't about World War II; it was about the War for the Ring. If there are any politics being reflected in my books, it's the politics of the Hundred Years War, and the Crusades, and the Wars of the Roses.'[15] In another interview, he'd be even more blunt: 'My work is not an allegory ... If I wanted to write about the financial crisis or the conflict in Syria, I would write about the financial crisis or the conflict in Syria, without any metaphor.'[16]

The question, then, is not whether George R.R. Martin intentionally uses his work to explore issues affecting contemporary readers; the question is whether it's possible to create a work of fantasy – or indeed any work of fiction – that doesn't in some way speak to the times in which it is published. It's become a cliché to say that science fiction and fantasy stories say more about the era of their creation than any fictional past or future, but it's also, in many cases, true – as Martin's contemporary, the great speculative author Kim Stanley Robinson says: 'You write science fiction and you're actually writing about the reality that we're truly in, and that's what novels ought to do.'[17]

**OPPOSITE**
Foreign occupation:
The US Army on patrol in Mosul, Iraq in 2007 (top); and Daenerys Targaryen (Emilia Clarke) with her Unsullied army

We've already looked at how the flight of the Wildlings into Westeros might have been inspired – consciously or otherwise – by the movement of refugee peoples across the Mexican border or the Mediterranean Sea. Similarly, events in Slaver's Bay – specifically, Daenerys's conquest of the desert city of Meereen and her struggle to maintain her grip on power – could be seen to echo the American-led invasions of Iraq and Afghanistan and the violent insurgencies that followed, all of which were taking place while Martin was writing.

In one area alone, Martin accepts the existence of an intentional parallel. He told the *New York Times* in 2018:

> The people in Westeros are fighting their individual battles over power and status and wealth, and those are so distracting them that they're ignoring the threat of 'winter is coming,' which has the potential to destroy all of them and to destroy their world. And there is a great parallel there to ... what I see this planet doing ... We're fighting over issues – important issues, mind you, foreign policy, domestic policy, civil rights, social responsibility, social justice – but while we're tearing ourselves apart ... there exists this threat of climate change, which ... really has the potential to destroy our world.[18]

And this idea of a world in decline echoes throughout *A Song of Ice and Fire*. Signs of it are everywhere, from the band of rogues that populate the once-noble Kingsguard to the dwindling of the Night's Watch, from the destruction Daenerys leaves in her wake to the 'affront to all the laws of gods and men'[19] that is the Red Wedding. Yes, wars have always raged across the known world, and from Martin's histories we learn that they were often bloody, often brutal. But there seems to be a particular quality to the War of Five Kings and the battles for Slaver's Bay that set them apart: a savagery, a complete absence of chivalry or honour. Is it possible that this reflects a certain sense at large in the real world that things are darkening,

that cynicism and cruelty are winning the fight against hope and optimism?

Another of Martin's remarks would seem to suggest so. Discussing the increasingly gloomy depictions of the future offered by much of recent science fiction, Martin told an interviewer: 'Of course I would prefer to be part of another world; a better world, but I can't. Perhaps winter is not coming only to Winterfell, but in the real world.'[20] Because, of course, *A Song of Ice and Fire* is not just a story of dragons and kings, it is – as Martin has repeatedly stressed – an exploration of how those things impact their world. If kings make mistakes, entire populations suffer; if dragons are unleashed, it's not just soldiers who die, but countless innocents as well. And as our own world grows ever more troubled, as mad kings perch upon the thrones of superpowers,[21] the symmetry between our reality and Martin's becomes harder to ignore. Though, as the author admits, the bleakness of his fiction only reflects reality: 'There are some people who read and want to believe in a world where the good guys win and the bad guys lose, and at the end they live happily ever after. That's not the kind of fiction that I write.'[22]

And yet, however dark his books get, there's always a sense of wonder in Martin's works that belies their grimness and brutality:

> People read fantasy to see the colours again. I think there's something in us that yearns for something more, more intense experiences ... somewhere in our heart of hearts we don't want to live the lives of quiet desperation Thoreau spoke about, and fantasy ... takes us to amazing places and shows us wonders. And that fulfils a need in the human heart.'[23]

Epilogue

# THE
# GARDENER

# 'Every man who walks the earth casts a shadow on the world'

Melisandre, *A Dance With Dragons*[1]

'Like every other young writer,' George R.R. Martin told the *Guardian* in 2018, 'I dreamed of fame and fortune. Having achieved them I can tell you that fortune is great ... [but] fame is definitely a double-edged sword.'[2] And yet, with the exception of J.K. Rowling and arguably Stephen King, George R.R. Martin is now the best-known author of fiction currently living – and, with his signature cap, beard and spectacles, he's more instantly recognizable than either. Which is both a blessing and a curse: 'the fans are usually very nice, but you can't control it, you can't turn it off. We all have bad days when we'd just like to be left alone.'[3]

From the very first episode of HBO's *Game of Thrones* back in 2011, George R.R. Martin's fate was sealed. Of course, he'd had fans before that: plenty of them, in fact, drawn by his short stories, his novels, his editorship of the *Wild Cards* series and his frequent appearances at sci-fi and fantasy conventions. But when that first episode scored 2.2 million viewers on the first night – enough for HBO to commission a second series based on those figures alone – everything changed. From that day on, George R.R. Martin would be known as the man who made fantasy not just mature and acceptable but dangerous, indulgent and even sexy.

Not that it had been an easy ride: indeed, Martin had written *A Game of Thrones* safe in the knowledge that filming it would be impossible. He told *Collider* in 2011:

> When I began this series, I thought, this could never be adapted ... Writing a book, you're not constrained by a budget. You're not constrained by what you can do in terms of the special effects ... I said, 'I'm just going to write the best book I can, and it's probably only ever going to be a book, but that's fine with me. I love books' ... [Studios] were looking at the success of *The Lord of the Rings* movies ... and thinking, well, if it happened for one fantasy, perhaps it could happen to another ... But I knew right from the start that it couldn't be done as a feature film. It's simply too big.[4]

It wasn't until 2006 that Martin finally met two potential producers whose vision seemed to align with his own. David Benioff and D.B. Weiss may not have been household names – Benioff was a respected screenwriter with titles such as Spike Lee's *25th Hour* (2002) and sword-and-sandal epic *Troy* (2004) behind him, while Weiss was essentially a newcomer – but over a lengthy lunch they impressed Martin, both with their enthusiasm and with their knowledge of his work (famously, he asked them who they thought Jon Snow's real mother was). 'I had a great feeling about them,' Martin would say later. 'You have to find people that you trust, and put your faith in them and in their understanding of the story.'[5]

On a handshake deal, Benioff and Weiss took their pitch to HBO. 'We loved the same classic HBO shows that everybody loved, and we knew that this fit in,' Weiss would tell *Vanity Fair*. 'It was just a question of convincing them.' 'We ended up writing them this letter,' Benioff adds. 'Explaining why this would work ... "This is what you guys do. Whether it's taking the cop show with *The Wire* or gangster shows with *The Sopranos* and making them dirty and reinventing them."'[6] HBO bit, and soon Martin had an official contract: 'I gave them the rights to adapt this as a television series, and I got certain titles,

an agreement that I'd write one script a year and a large dump truck full of money.'[7]

But even when they got the green light, the process was far from smooth. The first pilot – directed by indie filmmaker Tom McCarthy, whose *Spotlight* (2015) would win the Best Picture Oscar a few years later – was a disaster. Though most of the cast were in place, the script was flawed and, as Benioff and Weiss later admitted, key information wasn't getting across. 'That last scene, where Jaime and Cersei ... are making love – [the audience] didn't know that they were brother and sister,' Benioff recalled. 'Mike Lombardo, then-president of HBO, came in unannounced to watch the pilot ... And I was just staring at Mike's face. It was like a horror movie.'[8] Amazingly, HBO didn't ditch the show. Instead, they went ahead with a 10-episode order, including a near-total reshoot of the pilot. 'To be given the opportunity to do something like this one time is a pretty rare gift,' Weiss recalled. 'To be given the opportunity to do more or less the exact same thing twice is an extremely rare gift.'[9]

For a show with no major stars, a limited pre-existing fanbase and – at least for the first couple of seasons – a relatively small budget, the success of *Game of Thrones* still seems astonishing. The first season finale would draw in

**ABOVE**
George R.R. Martin
with the cast and crew
of *Game of Thrones* at
the Chinese Theatre
in Hollywood, 2013

**OPPOSITE**
Beard tales: GRRM
greets his fans at a
2014 book signing
in Dijon, France

# 'They pay him gold and silver, but he only gives them writing. Are they stupid?'

Arya Stark, *A Dance With Dragons*[10]

some 3 million viewers; by the final season premiere, that had rocketed to an astonishing 17.4 million. The first season was nominated for 13 Emmy awards, including Outstanding Drama Series; it took home two, including a Supporting Actor win for Peter Dinklage as Tyrion Lannister (he would also score a Golden Globe for the same role). Countless other garlands would follow, from the American Film Institute's coveted TV award to a near-sweep at the IGN People's Choice awards. Over its eight-season run, *Game of Thrones* would ultimately pick up an astonishing 59 Emmy awards – setting a new record in 2015 with 12 wins in a single year – alongside awards from bodies as diverse as the Screen Actors' Guild, the Peabody awards and the Hugos, and break Guinness World Records for Largest TV Drama Simulcast and (rather less gratifyingly) the Most Pirated TV Show of all time.

And the impact of the show was equally impossible to ignore, for better and worse. We've already looked at how the depiction of sexual violence sparked controversy in later seasons (see page 115), but that wasn't the case at first – indeed, while the wedding-night rape of Daenerys Targaryen may have made some viewers uncomfortable, many commentators found the show's frequent nudity, adult language and frank depiction of taboo topics like incest thrilling. It wasn't long before an entirely new word entered the TV critic's lexicon: 'sexposition', the art of sweetening scenes containing reams of necessary dialogue either by conducting them *in flagrante*, or by placing naked women in the background of every shot.

Of course, none of this was accidental. In 2012, director Neil Marshall recalled how, during the filming of the season 2 episode 'Blackwater', 'this particular [HBO executive] took me to one side and said, "Look, I represent the pervert side of the audience, okay? ... And I'm saying I want full-frontal nudity in this scene".'[11] More recently, Emilia Clarke told the Armchair Expert podcast how she felt a certain pressure to disrobe: 'I have had fights on set ... They're like "You don't want to disappoint your *Game of Thrones* fans." And I'm like, "Fuck you!"'[12]

But this wasn't the first TV epic to dish out full-frontal nudity: the 2005 series *Rome* is widely seen as a stage-setter for *Game of Thrones*, while *Spartacus: Blood and Sand* premiered in 2010 and was, if anything, even more salacious. But still, it wasn't long before every network began to take notice: the years following *Game of Thrones*' debut saw the arrival of shows as diverse as pirate adventure *Black Sails*

(first season 2014), time-travel romp *Outlander* (first season 2014), sci-fi western *Westworld* (first season 2016), women's prison comedy *Orange is the New Black* (first season 2013), 70s porn-scene exposé *The Deuce* (first season 2017) and high school drama *Euphoria* (first season 2019), each of which featured regular nudity, and many of which also used sexual violence as a plot device.

But perhaps the most direct offspring of *Game of Thrones* is *The Witcher* (first season 2019). Based on a series of novels by Polish author Andrzej Sapkowski – the first volume of which, *Blood of Elves*, was published in 1994, two years before *A Game of Thrones* – the Netflix show may lack the wit and complexity of its ancestor, but that hasn't stopped it from becoming enormously popular. And here we see a more positive result of *Game of Thrones*' success: the rise of epic fantasy as a bankable genre. That process had begun a decade earlier with the release of Peter Jackson's *The Lord of the Rings* film trilogy (2001–03), but *Game of Thrones* kicked things into high gear, spurring an ongoing boom in fantasy television that includes several shows – *Outlander* (2014–present), *The Wheel of Time* (2021–present), *His Dark Materials* (2019–22), *The Sandman* (2022–present), *The Shannara Chronicles* (2016–17) – based on book series by Martin's contemporaries. The headcount of fantasy (or, like *Vikings*, 2013–20, fantasy-adjacent) shows produced since 2011 is too long to list in full, but just a few would be *Britannia* (2018–21), *The Dark Crystal* (2019), *The Last Kingdom* (2015–22), *Cursed* (2020), *Shadow and Bone* (2021–23) and, of course, Amazon's billion-dollar gamble *The Rings of Power* (2022–present), which debuted in 2022 alongside HBO's first *Game of Thrones* spin-off series, *House of the Dragon* (2022–present).

Set approximately two centuries before the events of *A Song of Ice and Fire*, *House of the Dragon* draws largely on Martin's own written history of the Targaryen dynasty, *Fire and Blood* (2018). But though it was the first such series to reach our screens, it wasn't the first to be planned, or even shot. HBO had been discussing potential spin-off ideas

The cast of *Game of Thrones* with just a few of their many Emmy awards, Los Angeles, 2018

Children of Thrones:
some of the many
historical and/or
fantastical shows
to spring up in
the wake of GoT.
On the opposite page:
*Outlander* (top left);
*Black Sails* (top right);
*Cursed* (middle left);

*The Last Kingdom*
(middle right) and
*The Witcher* (bottom).
On this page: *The Lord
of the Rings: The Rings
of Power* (top); *His Dark
Materials* (middle left);
*The Sandman* (middle
right) and *The Wheel
of Time* (bottom).

since *Game of Thrones* debuted, and in 2019 went as far as to shoot the pilot for a series provisionally entitled *The Long Night*, set during the first war against the White Walkers. With a pointedly female-fronted cast and crew – stars Naomi Watts and Denise Gough, showrunner Jane Goldman and director S.J. Clarkson – the pilot was nonetheless deemed a failure and was shelved in favour of the more audience-friendly *House of the Dragon*.

But perhaps the biggest impact made by *Game of Thrones* was on George R.R. Martin's sales figures – with over 90 million books sold, *A Song of Ice and Fire* is now the second most popular fantasy series of all time behind *The Lord of the Rings*.[13] But a rising tide lifts all boats, and the boom in fantasy television has been mirrored by the regular presence of fantasy novels on the bestseller lists: Patrick Rothfuss's *Kingkiller Chronicles* (2007–11), N.K. Jemisin's *The Broken Earth* trilogy (2015–17) and Brandon Sanderson's *Mistborn* series (2006–present) have all surely benefited from the *Game of Thrones* effect, as have the sales of countless pre-existing fantasy classics.

And yet, the fact that by its fifth season events in the HBO series had begun to outpace those in its parent novels was troubling, not least to George R.R. Martin. As late as 2013, he'd still been expecting to be able to complete *A Song of Ice and Fire* before the TV show caught up: 'my dream chronology is that the books finish first. It's true that they're moving faster than I am ... but I don't see us catching up for another three years or so, by which time another book will be out.'[14] There were even plans made for a hiatus in the show, a break of a year or two to allow Martin to catch up. But that wasn't how things worked out: the sixth book has still to arrive, while the demands of series television meant that *Game of Thrones* needed to be concluded. 'I wish I had stayed ahead,' Martin told a Chicago audience in 2021. '[But] they caught up with me and passed me, and that made it a little strange because now the show was ahead of me and going in different directions.'[15]

Though later seasons were ostensibly based on outlines provided by Martin, many of the decisions that Benioff and Weiss took still proved controversial. And although Martin has remained largely close-mouthed on the matter, we do know that a lot of those choices were made without his express consent – 'by season five and six, and certainly seven and eight, I was pretty much out of the loop,' he told the *New York Times*[16] – and that the ending of the show will not be the same in the books. 'How will it all end? I hear people asking,' he wrote on his blog. 'The same ending as the show? Different? Well ... yes.  And no. And yes. And no. And yes. And no. And yes.'[17]

In truth, the books had already taken a different tack even before the show overtook them: the presence in *A Dance With Dragons* of characters like the Ironborn captain Victarion Greyjoy, Young Griff a.k.a. the disguised Targaryen heir, Aegon VI, and, of course, the resurrected and vengeful Lady Stoneheart meant that any close mirroring was already impossible. We also know, from comparing Martin's original 1993 outline with the books that eventually emerged, that his initial ideas tend to be significantly altered by the time they reach the page: the striking difference between that rough draft and its ultimate realization suggest that any notes that Martin gave to Benioff and Weiss could easily be old hat by the time he comes to write his finale.

As the years go by, there are some fans who grow increasingly restless at Martin's apparent lack of progress: 'whenever I blogged about going on a trip or a vacation ... that would always trigger a wave of how dare you do that, finish the book, that's your main obligation,' he mourns.[18] But there are many more who are willing to bide their time, who understand that Martin is still working on the book set to be called *The Winds of Winter* – but that he's also busy with many other projects, not to mention taking some well-earned time to enjoy the fruits of his labours.

Because the truth is that even George R.R. Martin doesn't know exactly where this story is going to end up, how long it'll take, and how many of his characters will survive. 'I think there are two types of writers, the architects and the gardeners,' he said in 2011, expounding on a favourite theme:

> The architects plan everything ahead of time ... they have the whole thing designed and blueprinted out before they even nail the first board up. The gardeners dig a hole, drop in a seed ... They know if they planted a fantasy seed or a mystery seed or whatever. But as the plant comes up and they water it, they don't know how many branches it's going to have, they find out as it grows. And I'm much more a gardener than an architect.[19]

All good things: the final episodes of *Game of Thrones*, as Daenerys (Emilia Clarke) surveys the devastation of King's Landing (top), while King Bran (Isaac Hempstead-Wright) and his sisters bid farewell to Jon Snow (Kit Harington) (bottom)

# Bibliography

**WORKS BY GEORGE R.R. MARTIN:**

*A Song of Ice and Fire:*
*A Game of Thrones,* Bantam Spectra,
New York, 1996.
*A Clash of Kings,* Voyager Books,
New York, 1998.
*A Storm of Swords,* Voyager Books, 2000.*
*A Feast for Crows,* Voyager Books, 2005.
*A Dance With Dragons,* Voyager Books, 2011.

*Page references in this book refer to the
two-volume UK paperback edition
of *A Storm of Swords,* published by
Voyager in 2001.

Other works:
*Dying of the Light,* Simon and Schuster,
New York, 1977.
*Fevre Dream,* Poseidon Press,
New York, 1982.
*The Armageddon Rag,* Poseidon Press,
New York, 1983.
*Dreamsongs: A RRetrospective,* Victor
Gollancz Ltd, London, 2006.
*The World of Ice and Fire* (with Elio M.
Garcia Jr and Linda Antonsson),
Bantam, New York, 2014.
*A Knight of the Seven Kingdoms,* Bantam
Books, New York, 2015.
*Fire and Blood,* Bantam Books,
New York, 2018.

**WORKS BY OTHERS:**

Larrington, Carolyne. *Winter is Coming,*
I.B. Tauris, London, 2016.
Larrington, Carolyne. *All Men Must Die,*
Bloomsbury Academic, London, 2021.
Lushkov, Ayelet Haimson. *You Win or You
Die,* I.B. Tauris, London, 2017.
Weinczok, David C. *The History Behind
Game of Thrones: The North
Remembers,* Pen & Sword History,
Barnsley, 2020.

**USEFUL WEBSITES:**

George RR Martin: The official GRRM
website, with informative sections
on his books, his obsessions and his
life story. (georgerrmartin.com)

Not a Blog: George RR Martin's own outlet
for news, reading recommendations,
ideas, thoughts and general ramblings.
(georgerrmartin.com/notablog/)
Westeros.org: The main fansite for
all things *A Song of Ice and Fire.*
(westeros.org)
A Wiki of Ice and Fire: Detailed articles
on every aspect of ASOIAF. (awoiaf.
westeros.org/index.php/Main_Page)

**ONLINE INTERVIEWS WITH
GEORGE R.R. MARTIN:**

Anders, Charlie Jane. 'George R.R. Martin
Answers Our Toughest *Song of Ice
and Fire* Questions', *Gizmodo,* 23
July 2013. (gizmodo.com/george-r-r-
martin-answers-our-toughest-song-
of-ice-and-886133300)
Cornwell, Bernard. 'Interview with George
R.R. Martin', *BernardCornwell.net.*
(bernardcornwell.net/interview-
with-george-r-r-martin/)
Dolin, Anton. '"Fantasy needs magic"
An interview with George R.R.
Martin', *Meduza,* 22 August 2017.
(meduza.io/en/feature/2017/08/22/
fantasy-needs-magic)
Flood, Alison. 'Getting more from
George R.R. Martin', *Guardian,*
14 April 2011. (theguardian.com/
books/booksblog/2011/apr/14/
more-george-r-r-martin)
Flood, Alison. 'George R.R. Martin:
*Game of Thrones* characters die
because "it has to be done"', *Guardian,*
17 May 2016. (theguardian.com/
books/2016/may/17/george-rr-martin-
game-of-thrones-characters-die-it-
has-to-be-done-song-of-ice-and-fire)
Flood, Alison. 'George R.R. Martin:
'When I began *A Game of Thrones* I
thought it might be a short story',
*Guardian,* 10 November 2018. (www.
theguardian.com/books/2018/nov/10/
books-interview-george-rr-martin)
Gentry, Amy. 'LoneStarCon 3: The
George R.R. Martin Interview',
*Austin Chronicle,* 29 August 2013.
(austinchronicle.com/daily/books/
2013-08-29/lonestarcon-3-the-george-
r-r-martin-interview/)

Gilmore, Mikal. 'George R.R. Martin:
The Rolling Stone Interview',
*Rolling Stone,* 23 April 2014.
(rollingstone.com/culture/culture-
news/george-r-r-martin-the-rolling-
stone-interview-242487/)
Glazer, Gwen. 'WWGRRMR: What
Would George R.R. Martin Read?'
*New York Public Library,* 26 June
2018. (nypl.org/blog/2018/06/26/
readingislit-grrm-books)
Goodrich, John. 'Famous Writers:
A Quick Interview With George
R.R. Martin', *Qusoor,* February 1999.
(qusoor.com/Essays/Martin.htm)
Guxens, Adria. 'George R.R. Martin: "Trying
to please everyone is a horrible
mistake"', *Adria's News,* 7 October 2012.
(adriasnews.com/2012/10/george-r-r-
martin-interview.html)
Itzkoff, Dave. 'George R.R. Martin on *Game
of Thrones* and Sexual Violence',
*New York Times Artsbeat,* 2 May 2014.
(archive.nytimes.com/artsbeat.blogs.
nytimes.com/2014/05/02/george-r-
r-martin-on-game-of-thrones-and-
sexual-violence/?smid=tw-share)
Hibberd, James. '*A Dance With Dragons*
Interview', *Entertainment Weekly,*
12 July 2011. (ew.com/article/2011/
07/12/george-martin-talks-a-dance-
with-dragons/)
Perry, Kevin E.G. 'George R.R. Martin:
"I don't understand how people can
come to hate so much something
that they once loved"', *Independent,*
28 May 2022. (independent.co.uk/
arts-entertainment/books/features/
george-rr-martin-interview-game-of-
thrones-b2088451.html#r3z-addoor)
Poniewozik, James. 'George R.R. Martin
Interview', *Time,* 15 April 2011.
(entertainment.time.com/2011/04/15/
george-r-r-martin-on-game-of-
thrones-from-book-to-tv/)
Radish, Christina. 'George R.R. Martin
Interview', *Collider,* 17 April 2011.
(collider.com/george-r-r-martin-
interview-game-of-thrones/)
Sims, Jamie. 'George R.R. Martin
Answers Times Staffers Most
Burning Questions', *The New York
Times,* 16 October 2018. (nytimes.
com/2018/10/16/t-magazine/
george-rr-martin-qanda-game-
of-thrones.html)
Yu, Charles. 'George R.R. Martin, Fantasy's
Reigning King', *The New York
Times,* 15 October 2018. (nytimes.
com/2018/10/15/t-magazine/george-
rr-martin-got-interview.html)

# Endnotes

Resources quoted in full in the bibliography (see pp.194–95) are given in an abbreviated format here.

## INTRODUCTION

1 *Dreamsongs*, p. 7.
2 Poniewozik.
3 Martin, George R.R. 'So Spake Martin: November 1998', *westeros.org.* (www.westeros.org/Citadel/SSM/Month/1998/11)
4 *A Dance With Dragons*, p. 452.
5 McDonald, Corey W. 'How George R.R. Martin's family history in Bayonne inspired this *Game of Thrones* character', *nj.com*, 21 November 2018. (www.nj.com/hudson/2018/11/george_rr_martin_mind_behind_game_of_thrones_makes.html)
6 *Dreamsongs*, p. 9.
7 *Dreamsongs*, p. 10.
8 *Dreamsongs*, p. 296.
9 Martin, George R.R. 'Life and Times: Bayonne', *GeorgeRRMartin.com.* (georgerrmartin.com/about-george/life-and-times/bayonne)
10 Goodrich.
11 Martin, George R.R. 'Oh, So True', *Not a Blog*, 26 February 2023. (georgerrmartin.com/notablog/2023/02/26/oh-so-true)
12 Gilmore.
13 *Dreamsongs*, p. 125.
14 *Dreamsongs*, p. 129.
15 *A Feast for Crows*, p. 292.
16 Yu.
17 Martin, George R.R. 'Life and Times: Dubuque', *GeorgeRRMartin.com.* (georgerrmartin.com/about-george/life-and-times/dubuque)
18 *Dreamsongs*, p. 564.
19 *Dreamsongs*, p. 775.
20 Gilmore.
21 Martin, George R.R. 'Quotes', *imdb.com.* (m.imdb.com/name/nm0552333/quotes)
22 Flood (2018).
23 Ibid.
24 Martin, George R.R., letter to his agent, Ralph Vinccinanza, October 1993. (thewertzone.blogspot.com/2015/02/this-early-outline-for-song-of-ice-and.html)
25 Gilmore.
26 Anders.
27 Gentry.
28 Eisenstein, Phyllis. 'Near the Frozen North, Where Dragons Awaken', *Chicago Sun-Times*, 11 August 1996. The fact that the author of this review was in fact a good friend of Martin's – he dedicated *A Storm of Swords* to her – has not gone unnoticed.
29 Perry, Steve. 'Adventure Drives Medieval-Style Fantasy', *The Oregonian*, 27 June 1999.
30 Guxens.
31 Anders.
32 Gentry.

## CHAPTER ONE

1 Guxens.
2 *A Game of Thrones*, p. 177.
3 Hanson, Marilee. 'Hadrian's Wall', *English History*, 29 April 2022. (englishhistory.net/romans/hadrians-wall)
4 *A Feast for Crows*, p. 185. The archmaester's name is a reference to Robert Jordan, author of the *Wheel of Time* series, whose given name is James Oliver Rigney, Jr.
5 Lobell, Jarrett A. 'The Wall at the End of the Empire'. *Archaeology*, May–June 2017, pp. 26–35.
6 *Dreamsongs*, p. 353.
7 *A Dance With Dragons*, p. 146.
8 Glazer. The others, for those interested, were *The Lord of the Rings* (1954–55), *The Great Gatsby* (1925), *Catch-22* (1961) and *The Prince of Tides* (1986).
9 Smith, Corey. 'George R.R. Martin raves about *War Lord*, the final *Saxon Stories* novel', *Winter is Coming*, 23 November 2020. (winteriscoming.net/2020/11/23/george-r-r-martin-endorses-bernard-cornwells-final-saxon-stories-novel-war-lord)
10 Martin, George R.R. 'Reading Recommendations', *Not a Blog*, 13 March 2013. (grrm.livejournal.com/316785.html)
11 Martin, George R.R. 'My Hero: Maurice Druon', *Guardian*, 5 April 2013. (www.theguardian.com/books/2013/apr/05/maurice-druon-george-rr-martin)
12 Ibid.
13 Ibid.
14 Larrington, Carolyne, 'George R.R. Martin's *A Song of Ice and Fire* and Maurice Druon's *Les Rois Maudits* (*The Accursed Kings*)' from Larrington, C. and Czarnowus, A. (eds), *Memory and Medievalism in George R.R. Martin and* Game of Thrones, Bloomsbury Academic, London, 2024, pp. 11–23.
15 Cornwell.
16 Gentry.
17 Gilmore.
18 Gentry.
19 Gilmore.
20 *A Game of Thrones*, p. 754.
21 *A Game of Thrones*, p. 119.
22 *A Clash of Kings*, p. 233.
23 *A Game of Thrones*, p. 233.
24 Preston, Richard E. '*Game of Thrones* as Myth: The Roots of the White Walkers', *Winter is Coming*, 2018. (winteriscoming.net/2017/07/15/game-of-thrones-as-myth-the-roots-of-the-white-walkers-the-others)
25 In the show, of course, the White Walkers were created by the Children of the Forest to drive humanity out of Westeros – a very *Sidhe*-like ambition.
26 Larrington (2016), p. 85.
27 *Dreamsongs*, p. 351.
28 'An Evening with George R.R. Martin and Kim Stanley Robinson', Arthur C. Clarke Center for Human Imagination, 27 May 2017. (www.youtube.com/watch?v=zfbwx7RAJss&t=0s)
29 Quoted in *Dreamsongs*, p. 358.

## CHAPTER TWO

1 Uncredited author, 'Arundel castle', *1066.co.nz.* (www.1066.co.nz/Mosaic%20DVD/whoswho/text/Arundel_Castle[1].htm)
2 *A Feast for Crows*, p. 375.
3 *Fire and Blood*, p. 344.
4 *A Game of Thrones*, p. 75.
5 Ibid.
6 Peake, Mervyn. *Titus Groan*, Eyre & Spottiswoode, London, 1946, p. 135. The appearance of the word *stark* in this brief quotation is almost certainly coincidental.
7 Martin, George R.R. 'Reading Recommendations', *Not a Blog*, 13 March 2013. (grrm.livejournal.com/316785.html)

8    Gentry.

9    Gilmore.

10   *A Clash of Kings*, p. 45.

11   Hall, Edward, quoted in Morris, Sylvia, 'Rehabilitating Shakespeare's "she-wolf of France", Margaret of Anjou', *The Shakespeare Blog*, 31 May 2018. (theshakespeareblog.com/2018/05/rehabilitating-shakespeares-she-wolf-of-france-margaret-of-anjou)

12   Martin, George R.R. 'So Spake Martin: November 1998', *westeros.org*. (www.westeros.org/Citadel/SSM/Month/1998/11)

13   Cornwell.

14   *A Game of Thrones*, p. 93.

15   *A Storm of Swords Part 1*, p. 328.

16   Unknown author, *The Battle of Maldon*, written 991–1066, lines 17–20. (english.nsms.ox.ac.uk/oecoursepack/maldon/translations/killingsfull.htm)

17   Gilmore.

18   *A Storm of Swords Part 2*, p. 171.

19   Schmidt, Ondřej. *John of Moravia between the Czech Lands and the Patriarchate of Aquileia (c. 1345–1394)*, Brill, Leiden, Netherlands, 2019, p. 22.

20   Bausells, Marta. 'George R.R. Martin in quotes: "I love writing about bastards"', *Guardian*, 11 August 2014. (www.theguardian.com/books/2014/aug/11/george-rr-martin-in-quotes-i-love-writing-about-bastards)

**CHAPTER THREE**

1    *The World of Ice and Fire*, p. 176.

2    *A Clash of Kings*, p. 154.

3    *A Clash of Kings*, p. 487.

4    *A Clash of Kings*, p. 131.

5    Martin, George R.R. 'So Spake Martin: January 1999', *westeros.org*. (www.westeros.org/Citadel/SSM/Month/1999/01)

6    *Fire and Blood*, p. 146.

7    *A Feast for Crows*, p. 23.

8    Martin, George R.R. 'Reading Recommendations', *Not a Blog*, 13 March 2013. (grrm.livejournal.com/316785.html)

9    *A Feast for Crows*, p. 22.

10   *The World of Ice and Fire*, p. 175.

11   Martin, George R.R. 'So Spake Martin: November 1998', *westeros.org*. (www.westeros.org/Citadel/SSM/Month/1998/11)

12   *A Dance With Dragons*, p. 286.

13   Larrington (2021), p. 146.

14   *A Feast for Crows*, p. 72.

15   *A Storm of Swords Part 1*, p. 348.

16   *A Clash of Kings*, p. 159.

17   Hibberd.

18   'George R. R. Martin: The World of Ice and Fire', *92NYPlus*, 27 October, 2014. (www.youtube.com/watch?v=Vcy-EhkHXnE&t=0s)

19   *A Clash of Kings*, p. 344.

20   Kosto, Adam J. *Hostages in the Middle Ages*, Oxford University Press, Oxford, 2012.

21   *A Feast for Crows*, p. 648.

22   Chadwick, Elizabeth. 'Biography of John Marshal', *Living History*, 11 October 2009. (livingthehistoryelizabethchadwick.blogspot.com/2009/10/biography-of-john-marshal.html)

23   Giebfried, John. 'Mortgaging Medieval Children', *Medievalists.net*. (www.medievalists.net/2019/01/mortgaging-medieval-children)

24   Larrington (2016), p. 120.

**CHAPTER FOUR**

1    Martin, George R.R. 'So Spake Martin: February 1999', *westeros.org*. (www.westeros.org/Citadel/SSM/Month/1999/02)

2    *A Game of Thrones*, p. 697.

3    Lister, Kate. 'The Bishop's Profitable Sex Workers in 14th-Century London', *Brewminate*, 23 November 2018. (brewminate.com/the-bishops-profitable-sex-workers-in-14th-century-london)

4    Ibid.

5    *A Game of Thrones*, p. 367.

6    *A Game of Thrones*, p. 44.

7    Clegg, Tom. 'Bawds, Pimps and Procurers: Images of the Prostitute in Medieval England', *Medieval History*, Issue 5, January 2004.

8    *A Clash of Kings*, pp. 535–536.

9    *A Feast for Crows*, p. 620.

10   Budiansky, Stephen. 'Sir Francis Walsingham', *Britannica.com*, 1999. (www.britannica.com/biography/Francis-Walsingham)

11   Ibid.

12   *A Clash of Kings*, p. 89.

13   Uncredited author, 'Edward IV', *englishmonarchs.co.uk*. (www.englishmonarchs.co.uk/plantagenet_12.htm)

14   Hanson, Marilee. 'A contemporary description of Henry VIII, 1515', *English History*, 10 February 2015. (englishhistory.net/tudor/henry-viii-contemporary-description)

15   *Dreamsongs*, p. 122.

16   *A Clash of Kings*, p. 317.

17   Perry, Kevin E.G. 'George R.R. Martin: "*Game of Thrones* was pitched as *The Sopranos* in Middle Earth"', *Independent*, 14 May 2022. (www.independent.co.uk/arts-entertainment/tv/news/george-rr-martin-got-santa-fe-festival-b2089380.html)

18   'In Conversation with George R.R. Martin', *TIFF Originals*, 14 March 2012. (www.youtube.com/watch?v=3S51ioEANGA&t=0s)

19   The so-called 'Hand's tournament' in *A Game of Thrones* is the only full-scale medieval-style tournament in the books thus far, though we also read of several smaller affairs, such as Joffrey's name-day tourney and Renly's melee battle at Bitterbridge, at which Brienne of Tarth wins the right to join his Rainbow Guard.

20   Larrington (2016), p. 121.

21   *A Clash of Kings*, p. 262.

22   *A History of Ice and Fire*, p. 50.

23   *A Dance With Dragons*, p. 878.

24   Good, Jonathan. 'Review of Shame and Honor: A Vulgar History of the Order of the Garter', *Reviews in History*, October 2013. (reviews.history.ac.uk/review/1495)

25   *A Clash of Kings*, p. 261.

26   Martin, George R.R. 'Knights', *GeorgeRRMartin.com*. (georgerrmartin.com/for-fans/knights)

27   Martin, George R.R. 'Courtenay and his Heirs', *GeorgeRRMartin.com*. (georgerrmartin.com/for-fans/knights/courtenay-and-his-heirs)

28   Martin, George R.R. 'The Knights of the Seven Kingdoms', *GeorgeRRMartin.com*. (georgerrmartin.com/for-fans/knights/the-knights-of-the-seven-kingdoms)

29   Martin, George R.R. 'Knights', *GeorgeRRMartin.com*. (georgerrmartin.com/for-fans/knights)

**CHAPTER FIVE**

1   Preston, Richard E. 'The Anarchy: The real war that inspired *House of the Dragon*', *Winter is Coming*, 13 August 2022. (winteriscoming. net/2022/08/13/the-anarchy-the-real-war-inspired-george-r-r-martin-house-of-the-dragon)

2   *House of the Dragon* episode 1.2, 'The Rogue Prince'.

3   *A Dance With Dragons*, p. 160.

4   Ryan, Maureen. 'The Most Important Conversation about Nuclear Weapons is Happening on '*House of the Dragon*', *Outrider*, Oct 3, 2022. (www.outrider.org/nuclear-weapons/articles/most-important-conversation-about-nuclear-weapons-happening-house-dragon)

5   *A Storm of Swords Part 2*, p. 204.

6   *A Storm of Swords Part 2*, p. 4.

7   *A Storm of Swords Part 2*, p. 405.

8   Uncredited author. 'Crusaders massacre of Jerusalem was done in cold-blood, not religious frenzy, historian argues', *Medievalists.net*. (www.medievalists.net/2011/01/crusaders-massacre-of-jerusalem-was-done-in-cold-blood-not-religious-frenzy-historian-argues)

9   *A Game of Thrones*, p. 780.

10  Blistein, Jon. 'George R.R. Martin Admits His Dragons Couldn't Beat Tolkien's Smaug in a Fight', *Rolling Stone*, 28 October 2014. (www.rollingstone.com/culture/culture-news/george-r-r-martin-admits-his-dragons-couldnt-beat-tolkiens-smaug-in-a-fight-73272/amp)

11  Uncredited author, 'Guillermo del Toro Gives Hobbit Update', *ComingSoon.net*, 12 November 2008. (www.comingsoon.net/movies/news/50460-guillermo-del-toro-gives-hobbit-update)

12  Although not covered extensively in this volume, movies are another key source of inspiration for George R.R. Martin - indeed, in 2013 he took ownership of an entire film theatre in his adopted home town of Santa Fe. The Jean Cocteau Cinema is still going strong, hosting not just movie screenings but author events, live shows and stand-up comedy. Find it at jeancocteaucinema.com.

13  'The Movie God'. '*Game Of Thrones* Author George R.R. Martin's Top Ten Favorite Fantasy Movies', *Geeks of Doom*, 16 April 2011. (geeksofdoom. com/2011/04/16/game-of-thrones-author-george-r-r-martins-top-ten-favorite-fantasy-movies)

14  Gilmore. The friend in question was, of course, the writer Phyllis Eisenstein, who gave such a glowing review to *A Game of Thrones*, and to whom *A Storm of Swords* is dedicated.

15  *Dreamsongs*, p. 296.

16  *Dreamsongs*, p. 299.

17  *Dreamsongs*, pp. 299–300.

18  Gilmore.

19  Flood (2018).

20  Martin, George R.R. 'Reading Recommendations', *Not a Blog*, 13 March 2013. (grrm.livejournal. com/316785.html)

21  Goodrich.

22  Uncredited author. 'George R.R. Martin Steers a Six-Book Cavalcade', *amazon.com*, 1999. (Archived at: web.archive.org/web/19991013131915/cyberhaven.com/books/sciencefiction/martin.html)

**CHAPTER SIX**

1   Sharp-eyed readers will note that this section of the book is entitled 'The Crownlands', whereas The Twins lie somewhat further north, in the kingdom known as the Riverlands. Sadly, this volume does not have the space to cover each of the Seven Kingdoms individually, and it was decided that 'The Crownlands' was a more inspiring title for this section of the book than, say, 'The Middle'.

2   Yes, in the books Catelyn does appear to have been resurrected by the Lord of Light and assumed the name Lady Stoneheart – but she was nonetheless murdered first.

3   *A Storm of Swords Part 1*, p. 458.

4   *A Dance With Dragons*, p. 511

5   'clark'. 'Xenia in The Odyssey: Manners Were Mandatory in Ancient Greece', *Classical Literature*, 11 January 2022. (ancient-literature. com/xenia-in-the-odyssey)

6   Ibid.

7   *A Storm of Swords Part 1*, p. 102.

8   Lambert, Tom. 'Hospitality, protection and refuge in early English law', *University of Oxford, Refugee Studies Centre*, 25 February 2015. (www.rsc.ox.ac.uk/events/hospitality-protection-and-refuge-in-early-english-law)

9   Mair, George. 'George R.R. Martin reveals Edinburgh Castle inspiration for bloody *Game of Thrones* Red Wedding scene'. *Edinburgh News*, 9 February 2020. (www.edinburghnews. scotsman.com/whats-on/arts-and-entertainment/george-rr-martin-reveals-edinburgh-castle-inspiration-bloody-game-thrones-red-wedding-scene-1393905)

10  Weinczok, p. 294.

11  Ibid.

12  *A Clash of Kings*, p. 683

13  Uncredited author. 'Glencoe National Nature Reserve', *National Trust for Scotland*. (www.nts.org.uk/visit/places/glencoe/the-glencoe-massacre)

14  Martin, George R.R. 'Quotes', *imdb.com*. (www.imdb.com/name/nm0552333/quotes)

15  Flood (2016).

16  Gilmore.

17  Cain, Sian. 'George R.R. Martin's teenage fan letter to Stan Lee: "A masterpiece – with one flaw"', *Guardian*, 20 July 2016. (www. theguardian.com/books/2016/jul/20/george-rr-martin-stan-lee-fan-latter-fantastic-four-marvel)

18  *Dreamsongs*, p. 11.

19  Perry.

**CHAPTER SEVEN**

1   Martin, George R.R. 'A Couple of Rocks', *Not a Blog*, 23 December 2022. (georgerrmartin.com/notablog/2022/12/23/a-couple-of-rocks)

2   Ibid.

3   Ibid.

4   In the HBO series, Tywin implied that the mines of Casterly Rock had run dry, but as far as we know this is not the case in the books.

5   Martin, George R.R. 'A Few Words from Switzerland', *Not a Blog*, 30 August 2014. (grrm.livejournal. com/381419.html)

6   Martin, George R.R. 'So Spake Martin: Boskone (Boston, MA; February 17–19)', *westeros.org*. (www.westeros. org/Citadel/SSM/Entry/1436)

7   *A Game of Thrones*, p. 130.

8   *A Game of Thrones*, p. 54.

9    Crow, David. 'The Real History of *Game of Thrones*: Tyrion Lannister', *Den of Geek*, 17 May 2019. (www. denofgeek.com/tv/the-real-history-of-game-of-thrones-tyrion-lannister)

10   *A Clash of Kings*, p. 288.

11   Hall, Matthew T. 'If George R.R. Martin were in *Game of Thrones*, this is how he'd die', *San Diego Union-Tribune*, 28 July 2014. (www.sandiegouniontribune. com/opinion/the-conversation/sdut-george-rr-martin-comic-con-2014jul28-story.html)

12   Later in the book, Daenerys's treatment by Drogo becomes more problematic, as he wakes her every night to have rough sex with her, whether she wants to or not.

13   'Tafkar'. 'Rape in *ASOIAF* vs. *Game of Thrones*: a statistical analysis', *tafkarfanfic*, 24 May 2015. (tafkarfanfic.tumblr.com/ post/119770640640/rape-in-asoiaf-vs-game-of-thrones-a-statistical)

14   *A Storm of Swords Part 1*, p. 431.

15   Itzkoff.

16   'RibaldRemark'. 'A Response to George R.R. Martin's Interview', *The Critical Dragon*, 29 October 2015. (thecriticaldragon.com/2015/10/29/ a-response-to-george-r-r-martins-interview).

17   *A Dance With Dragons*, p. 747.

18   Hibberd, James. '*Game of Thrones* producers: "Not one word" changed due to criticism', *Entertainment Weekly*, 1 April 2016. (ew.com/ article/2016/04/01/game-thrones-season-6)

19   Sephton, J. (translator). *Erik the Red's Saga*, D. Marples & Co., Liverpool, 1880.

20   Martin, George R.R. 'So Spake Martin: January 1999', *westeros.org*. (www.westeros.org/Citadel/SSM/ Month/1999/01)

21   *A Clash of Kings*, p. 312.

22   *A Clash of Kings*, p. 508.

23   Larrington (2016), p. 32.

24   A scene in *The Faerie Queene* in which a brazen noblewoman known as the Lady of Delight attempts to seduce Britomart and her male companions might also have inspired another classic work of fantastical medievalism (and another George R.R. Martin favourite), *Monty Python and the Holy Grail* (1975).

25   *A Clash of Kings*, p. 312.

**CHAPTER EIGHT**

1    Lipscomb, Suzannah. 'Why Did Anne Boleyn Have to Die?', *BBC History Magazine*. Vol. 14, no. 4, April 2013. pp. 18–24.

2    *A Storm of Swords Part 2*, p. 342.

3    *A Game of Thrones*, p. 38.

4    *A Clash of Kings*, p. 317.

5    Martin, George R.R. 'George R.R. Martin on *The Great Gatsby* from PBS' Great American Read', Double P Media, 20 September 2018. (www.youtube.com/ watch?v=TI6TAB9yYXE)

6    Glazer.

7    Salmose, Niklas. 'Reading Nostalgia: Textual Memory in *The Great Gatsby*', *The F. Scott Fitzgerald Review*, Penn State University Press, Volume 12, 2014. pp. 67–87.

8    'George R.R. Martin on *The Great Gatsby* from PBS', as above.

9    *A Clash of Kings*, p. 317.

10   *A Storm of Swords Part 2*, p. 444.

11   *A Feast for Crows*, p. 12.

12   *A Feast for Crows*, p. 14.

13   Arnold, Matthew. 'Thyrsis', 1865.

14   *A Feast for Crows*, p. 57.

15   Dolin.

16   *A Game of Thrones*, p. 118.

17   Le Guin, Ursula. *A Wizard of Earthsea*, Parnassus Press, California, US, 1968. p. 20.

18   *Fire and Blood*, p. 304.

19   *A Feast for Crows*, p. 93.

20   Dolin.

21   Austen, Jane. *Pride and Prejudice*, T. Egerton, London, 1813, p. 32.

22   Salinger, J.D. *The Catcher in the Rye*, Little, Brown and Company, Boston, 1951. p. 22.

**CHAPTER NINE**

1    *A Feast for Crows*, p. 214.

2    Anders.

3    Guxens.

4    *A Storm of Swords Part 1*, p. 520.

5    *A Storm of Swords Part 2*, p. 397.

6    Reiner, Rob (director). *The Princess Bride*, 1987, Twentieth Century Fox.

7    Guxens.

8    *The World of Ice and Fire*, p. 45.

9    *A Dance With Dragons*, p. 749.

10   *Fire and Blood*, p. 33.

11   Uncredited author. 'Poisoning in Ancient Times', Edinburgh Medical School, date unknown. (web.archive. org/web/20070321025053/www. portfolio.mvm.ed.ac.uk/studentwebs/ session2/group12/ancient.htm)

12   Maitland, Karen. 'Medieval Murder – Ten Handy Ways to Poison Your Spouse', *The History Girls*, 8 June 2016. (the-history-girls.blogspot. com/2016/06/medieval-murder-ten-handy-ways-to.html)

13   The similarity between 'Lysa' and 'Lys' would seem to be coincidental.

14   Poniewozik.

15   *A Storm of Swords Part 2*, p. 149. Tywin is obviously being a bit obtuse here – many more than 12 people died at the Red Wedding, not just in the hall itself but in the castle and the camps beyond.

16   *A Clash of Kings*, p. 553.

17   *A Game of Thrones*, p. 48.

18   Gilmore.

19   *A Storm of Swords Part 1*, p. 336.

**CHAPTER TEN**

1    *A Feast for Crows*, p. 103.

2    *A Feast for Crows*, p. 572.

3    *Fire and Blood*, p. 258.

4    *A Feast for Crows*, p. 275.

5    *The World of Ice and Fire*, p. 274.

6    *A Dance With Dragons*, p. 588.

7    Larrington (2016), p. 152.

8    *The World of Ice and Fire*, p. 274.

9    *A Storm of Swords Part 2*, p. 210.

10   *The World of Ice and Fire*, p. 275.

11   Panek, LeRoy Lad. *An Introduction to the Detective Story*, Bowling Green State University Popular Press, Bowling Green, Ohio, US, 1987, p. 78.

12   Martin, George R.R. 'Reading Recommendations', *Not a Blog*, 13 March 2013. (grrm.livejournal. com/316785.html)

13   *A Dance with Dragons*, p. 311.

14   *A Feast for Crows*, p. 210.

15   Ibid.

16   'George R.R. Martin visiting SF-Bokhandeln', *SFBokhandeln*, 23 June 2015. (www.youtube.com/ watch?v=OMvFNaqSWE0&t=1062s)

17   Martin, George R.R. 'Well Played', *Not a Blog*, 27 December 2020. (georgerrmartin.com/ notablog/2020/12/27/well-played)

18   Ibid.

19    Martin, George R.R. 'The Computer Was a Fish', *Analog*, August 1971.
20    Martin, George R.R. 'Well Played', *Not a Blog*, 27 December 2020.

**CHAPTER ELEVEN**

1    Martin, George R.R. 'Yakkity Yak (comments)', *Not a Blog*, 3 February 2012. (grrm.livejournal.com/263800.html)
2    *A Game of Thrones*, p. 733.
3    *A Clash of Kings*, p. 388.
4    Lane, George. 'Genocide and Crimes Against Humanity: Genghis Khan', *Academia*, 6 February 2009. (www.academia.edu/26802318/Genocide_and_Crimes_Against_Humanity_Khan_Genghis)
5    All above quotes derive from a translation of surviving parts of the Yassa by the seventeenth-century French interpreter, François Pétis de la Croix, quoted in American novelist and historian Harold Lamb's *Genghis Khan: The Emperor of All Men* (Robert M. McBride, New York, 1927). Given such a tortuous history, any such quotes should be taken – like every report on Temüjin's life and times – with a pinch of salt, and indeed many historians claim that Genghis Khan, despite his apparent religious tolerance, could – when it suited him – use religion as a pretext for the murder of his foes.
6    *A Game of Thrones*, p. 377.
7    *The World of Ice and Fire*, p. 289.
8    *A Game of Thrones*, p. 378.
9    Uncredited author. 'Silk Roads Programme: Mongolia', *unesco.org*. (en.unesco.org/silkroad/countries-alongside-silk-road-routes/mongolia)
10    *A Game of Thrones*, p. 378.
11    *A Game of Thrones*, p. 379.
12    Martin, George R.R. 'Yakkity Yak (comments)', *Not a Blog*, 3 February 2012. (grrm.livejournal.com/263800.html)
13    *A Game of Thrones*, p. 96.
14    Devereaux, Bret. 'Collections: That Dothraki Horde, Part IV: Screamers and Howlers', *A Collection of Unmitigated Pedantry*, 8 January 2021. (acoup.blog/2021/01/08/collections-that-dothraki-horde-part-iv-screamers-and-howlers)
15    Ibid.

**CHAPTER TWELVE**

1    Said, Edward. *Orientalism*, Pantheon Books, New York, US, 1978.
2    Larrington (2016), p. 222.
3    *A Storm of Swords Part 1*, p. 315.
4    Ringrose, Kathryn M. *The Perfect Servant: Eunuchs and the Social Construction of Gender in Byzantium*, University of Chicago Press, Chicago, US, 2007, p. 3.
5    Bond, Sarah. 'What *Game of Thrones* Gets Right and Wrong About Eunuchs and Masculinity', *Forbes*, 20 August 2017. (www.forbes.com/sites/drsarahbond/2017/08/20/what-game-of-thrones-gets-right-and-wrong-about-eunuchs-and-masculinity/?sh=3e8bfcb8c55f)
6    Battis, Jes. 'How Medieval are the Eunuchs in *Game of Thrones*?', *The Public Medievalist*, 14 November 2019. (publicmedievalist.com/got-eunuchs)
7    *A Dance With Dragons*, p. 26.
8    Battis, Jes. 'How Medieval are the Eunuchs in *Game of Thrones*?', *The Public Medievalist*, 14 November 2019. (publicmedievalist.com/got-eunuchs)
9    Quoted in Bond, as previous.
10    *The World of Ice and Fire*, p. 308.
11    *A Clash of Kings*, p. 11.
12    *A Storm of Swords Part 1*, p. 484.
13    Harvey, P.D.A. *Medieval Maps*, British Library, 1991.
14    Dempsey, Caitlin. 'A Brief Look at Medieval Maps and Travel Guides', *Geography Realm*, 26 November 2018. (www.geographyrealm.com/a-brief-look-at-medieval-maps-and-travel-guides)
15    Dolin.
16    Guxens.
17    Quoted in Lea, Richard. 'Science fiction: the realism of the twenty-first century', *Guardian*, 7 August 2015. (www.theguardian.com/books/2015/aug/07/science-fiction-realism-kim-stanley-robinson-alistair-reynolds-ann-leckie-interview)
18    Sims.
19    *A Feast for Crows*, p. 276.
20    Guxens.
21    In the aforementioned *New York Times* interview with Jamie Sims, Martin actually compares former President Trump to King Joffrey, claiming that 'they have the same level of emotional maturity'.
22    Gilmore.
23    Flood (2018).

**EPILOGUE**

1    *A Dance With Dragons*, p. 380.
2    Flood (2018).
3    Ibid.
4    Radish.
5    Martin, George R.R. 'A Dance With Dragons: George R.R. Martin', *Talks at Google*, 7 August 2011. (www.youtube.com/watch?v=QTTW8M_etko)
6    Windolf, Jim. 'The Surprising Connection Between *Game of Thrones* and *Monty Python*', *Vanity Fair*, 24 March 2014. (www.vanityfair.com/hollywood/2014/03/game-of-thrones-benioff-weiss-interview)
7    'A Dance With Dragons: George R.R. Martin', as above.
8    Windolf, as previous.
9    Ibid.
10    *A Dance With Dragons*, p. 839.
11    Fitzpatrick, Kevin. '*Game of Thrones* Director Explains All the Rampant Nudity', *Screen Crush*, 6 June 2012. (screencrush.com/game-of-thrones-nudity)
12    Shepard, Dax (host). 'Emilia Clarke', *Armchair Expert*, 18 November 2019. (armchairexpertpod.com/pods/emilia-clarke)
13    Rowland, Rey. 'The Bestselling Fantasy Books of All Time', *Book Riot*, 2 March 2023. (bookriot.com/bestselling-fantasy-books)
14    O'Connell, Mikey. '*Game of Thrones* Writer George R.R. Martin Thinks His Books Will Outpace the Series', *Hollywood Reporter*, 29 March 2013. (www.hollywoodreporter.com/tv/tv-news/game-thrones-writer-george-r-431725)
15    Romean, Rachel. '*Game of Thrones* George R.R. Martin Teases Novels' Ending in the Most GRRM Way Possible', *CinemaBlend*, 29 June 2021. (www.cinemablend.com/television/2569653/game-of-thrones-george-rr-martin-teases-a-song-of-ice-and-fire-novels-ending)
16    Sims.
17    Martin, George R.R. 'An Ending', *Not a Blog*, 20 May 2019. (georgerrmartin.com/notablog/2019/05/20/an-ending)
18    Ibid.
19    Flood (2011).

# Index

# Picture Credits

The publishers would like to thank the institutions, picture libraries, and photographers for their kind permission to reproduce the works featured in this book. Every effort has been made to trace all copyright holders but if any have been inadvertently overlooked, the publishers would be pleased to make the necessary arrangements at the first opportunity.

Key: t = top; b = bottom; l = left; c = centre; r = right; and variations thereof.

**8 l** Susan Candelario/Alamy; **8 r** Paul Brown/Alamy Live News; **9** © HBO/FlixPix/Alamy; **11 tl** Texas Trio/John Aster; **11 tr** Bettmann/Getty Images; **11 b** Used by permission of Special Collections & University Archives, University of California, Riverside; **12 tl** Simon and Schuster/Private Collection/AF Fotografie; **12 tc** Avon Books/John Aster; **12 tr** Poseidon Press/Private Collection/AF Fotografie; **12 bl** Timescape Books/Roland Smithies/luped.com; **12 br** Poseidon Press/Private Collection/AF Fotografie; **14 tl** Baen Books/John Aster; **14 tr** © Adolphe Pierre-Louis/Albuquerque Journal/ZUMAPRESS.com/Alamy; **14 br** CBS via Getty Images; **15** SNAP/Entertainment Pictures/Alamy; **17 t** © HBO/PictureLux/The Hollywood Archive/Alamy; **17 b** © HBO/Cinematic/Alamy; **18 t** © HBO/Album/Alamy; 18 bl Voyager/Private Collection/AF Fotografie; **18 br** CBW/Alamy; **23 t** © HBO - Embassy Films/TCD/Prod.DB/Alamy; **23 b** Pete Stuart/Shuttrstock; **25 tl** Archive PL/Alamy; **25 tr** Timescape/Private Collection/AF Fotografie; **25 b** HombreDHojalata (CC BY-SA 3.0 DEED); **26** AFP via Getty Images; **29** Design Pics Inc/Alamy; **30** De Luan/Alamy; **31 l** Bibliothèque nationale de France; **31 r** Andy Thompson/Alamy; **33 t** © HBO/AJ Pics/Alamy; **33 b** © HBO/Kobal/Shutterstock; **35 tl** Pierce Archive LLC/Buyenlarge via Getty Images; **35 tr** Susmuffin (public domain); **35 b** PictureLux/The Hollywood Archive/Alamy; **36–37** Carlo Bollo/Alamy; **39 l** World History Archive/Alamy; **39 r** Philadelphia Museum of Art (public domain); **40 l** Reynal & Hitchcock/Private Collection/AF Fotografie; **40 r** Raymond Kleboe/Picture Post/Hulton Archive/Getty Images; **41** Bridgeman Images; **42 l** Universal History Archive/UIG/Bridgeman Images; **42 r** Artanisen (public domain); **45** © HBO/PictureLux/The Hollywood Archive/Alamy; **47 t** Chiswick Chap (public domain); **47 b** Bridgeman Images;

**48** Bibliothèque nationale de France; **49** © Chetham's Library/Bridgeman Images; **51** © HBO/Pictorial Press Ltd/Alamy; **53 t** © Christopher Wood Gallery, London, UK/Bridgeman Images; **53 b** © HBO/Cinematic/Alamy; **54** © United Artists/Cinematic/Alamy; **57 t** © HBO/LANDMARK MEDIA/Alamy; **57 b** © HBO/Maximum Film/Alamy; **58** From the British Library archive/Bridgeman Images; **59** From the British Library archive/Bridgeman Images; **60** Florilegius/Alamy; **61** © HBO/Maximum Film/Alamy; **62** Texianlive/Alamy; **63** Chronicle/Alamy; **65 t** Photo: © The Governing Body of Christ Church, Oxford, Christ Church MS 92, 68v; **65 b** Chabeo1 (CC BY-SA 4.0 DEED); **69** © HBO/LANDMARK MEDIA/Alamy; **70 t** Sunny Celeste/Alamy; **70 b** Chronicle/Alamy; **71** Walters Art Museum (CC BY-SA 3.0 DEED); **73** CPA Media Pte Ltd/Alamy; **74 tl** Colin Underhill/Alamy; **74 tc** Colin Underhill/Alamy; **74 tr** Colin Underhill/Alamy; **74 bl** Colin Underhill/Alamy; **74 bc** Colin Underhill/Alamy; **74 br** Colin Underhill/Alamy; **77 t** © HBO/LANDMARK MEDIA/Alamy; **77 b** © HBO/Media Associates/Alamy; **78** Diligent (public domain); **79** From the British Library archive/Bridgeman Images; **80 l** From the British Library archive/Bridgeman Images; **80 r** Crisco 1492 (public domain); **81** © HBO/LANDMARK MEDIA/Alamy; **82** © HBO/LANDMARK MEDIA/Alamy; **83** Universal Images Group North America LLC/DeAgostini/Alamy; **85 l** HBO/Good Banana/Album/Alamy; **85 r** The Picture Art Collection/Alamy; **87 t** © HBO/PictureLux/The Hollywood Archive/Alamy; **87 bl** From the British Library archive/Bridgeman Images; **87 br** Pictorial Press Ltd/Alamy; **88** Bibliothèque nationale de France; **90–91** incamerastock/Alamy; **92** robertharding/Alamy; **93** TCD/Prod.DB/Alamy; **94** Pyramid Books/Roland Smithies/luped.com; **95 l** Haywood Magee/Picture Post/Hulton Archive/Getty Images; **95 r** © WingNut Films/New Line Cinema/Collection Christophel/Alamy; **96 tl** Gnome Press, Inc./Private Collection/AF Fotografie; **96 tc** Panther Books/Roland Smithies/luped.com; **96 tr** Weird Tales/John Aster; **96 bl** Puffin Books/Roland Smithies/luped.com; **96 bc** Puffin Books/Roland Smithies/luped.com; **96 br** Puffin Books/Roland Smithies/luped.com; **97** Bettmann/Getty Images; **99** © HBO/BFA; **100 t** Jane Hobson/Shutterstock; **100 b** ArtVee (public domain); **102** DcoetzeeBot (public domain); **103** Richard Whitcombe/Shutterstock; **105** Shamley Productions/

**ABOUT THE AUTHOR**

Tom Huddleston is a freelance film
and TV writer whose work has appeared
in *The Guardian*, *Time Out* and *Little
White Lies*, among others. He is the author
of *The Worlds of Dune* and several sci-fi
and fantasy novels for younger readers,
including the acclaimed *FloodWorld*
trilogy. He currently lives in London.


**ACKNOWLEDGEMENTS**

Boundless gratitude once again to
John Parton, First of his Name, for asking
me to write this weighty tome, and to
Ser Laura Bulbeck of Quarto for her deeply
knowledgeable and enthusiastic editing
and picture research.
   A deep doff of the velvet cap to
the ultimate medieval loremaster,
Professor Carolyne Larrington, for her
very illuminating notes and extremely
encouraging words, and as always
many thanks to my Master of Coin,
Ella Diamond Kahn, and all at DKW.
   Thanks to George R.R. Martin for
writing such a remarkable series of
books in the first place, and to all the
fans, academics, journalists and writers
whose work I drew upon in the creation
of this one.
   And lastly but by no means leastly,
my undying love and fealty to Rosalind
of House Greatorex, breaker of chains and
mother of dragons – or at least one small,
fire-breathing monster.